Remember This?

People, Things and Events
FROM **1951** TO THE **PRESENT DAY**

UK EDITION

With thanks for additional research by Dale Barham, Nicola Gardiner and Janice Morton.

Baby names: Office of National Statistics.

Cover images: Mary Evans – Keystone Pictures USA/zumapress.com, Roger Mayne Archive, Marx Memorial Library.
Cover icons from rawpixel/Freepik.

Cover Design: Fanni Williams / thehappycolourstudio.com

The Milestone Memories series including this *Remember This?* title is produced by Milestones Memories Press, a division of Say So Media Ltd.

First edition: October 2021
Updated: January 2022

We've tried our best to check our facts, but mistakes can still slip through. Spotted one? We'd love to know about it: info@saysomedia.net

Rewind, Replay, Remember

What can you remember before you turned six? If you're like most of us, not much: the comforting smell of a blanket or the rough texture of a sweater, perhaps. A mental snapshot of a parent arriving home late at night. A tingle of delight or the shadow of sorrow.

But as we grow out of childhood, our autobiographical and episodic memories – they're the ones hitched to significant events such as birthdays or leaving school – are created and filed more effectively, enabling us to piece them together at a later date. And the more we revisit those memories, the less likely we are to lose the key that unlocks them.

These fragments are assembled into a more-or-less coherent account of our lives – the one we tell ourselves, our friends, our relatives. And while this one-of-a-kind biopic loses a little definition over the years, some episodes remain in glorious technicolour – although it's often the most embarrassing incidents!

But this is one movie that's never quite complete. Have you ever had a memory spring back unbidden, triggered by something seemingly unrelated? This book is an attempt to discover those forgotten scenes using the events, sounds, and faces linked to the milestones in your life.

It's time to blow off the cobwebs and see how much you can remember!

It Happened in 1951

The biggest event in the year is one that didn't make the front pages: you were born! Here are some of the national stories that people were talking about.

✦ UK's largest oil refinery opens at Fawley near Southampton
✦ Britain abandons financial fiasco Tanganyika Groundnuts Scheme
✦ Spies Guy Burgess and Donald Maclean defect to USSR (right)
✦ General Certificate of Education O- and A-levels introduced
✦ Festival of Britain held countrywide to boost post-war morale
✦ New X rating introduced for films suitable for aged 16-plus
✦ UK's first zebra crossing installed in Slough
✦ First Miss World pageant held in London won by Miss Sweden
✦ Submarine HMS Affray sinks – all 75 crew lost
✦ 6,000 British troops flown to Suez Canal to suppress civil unrest
✦ Port Talbot steelworks open in Margam, south Wales
✦ Snowdonia designated Britain's third national park
✦ UK's first residential tower block built in Harlow, Essex
✦ Stolen Stone of Destiny returned to Westminster Abbey
✦ Tory Party led by Churchill wins general election
✦ Pool of London first British film with black actor in leading role
✦ Dennis the Menace makes his comic debut in The Beano
✦ Scotland's Beinn Eighe becomes UK's first National Nature Reserve
✦ Ealing crime caper The Lavender Hill Mob opens in cinemas
✦ John Wyndham's sci-fi novel The Day of the Triffids published
✦ The Goons Show makes its surreal debut on BBC radio

Born this year:
⚬ Musician Sting born Gordon Sumner in Wallsend, Tyneside
⚬ Husky-voiced singer Bonnie Tyler born Gaynor Hopkins near Swansea
⚬ Labour MP and PM Gordon Brown born near Glasgow
⚬ British singer and drummer Phil Collins born in London

The decrypted Soviet messages were clear: a KGB spy codenamed Homer was at work in UK diplomatic circles. The net was closing around the Cambridge Five, and in May 1951, Guy Burgess drove a hire car to the Kent home of Donald Maclean, introducing himself to Maclean's American wife Melinda as 'Roger Styles', and the pair drove off into the night to catch a ferry to France. They weren't seen again until a 1956 press conference in Moscow.

As rewards were offered for information about the pair, Melinda continued to play her role as the demure, deceived wife, abandoned weeks before she bore his third child. The press attention was relentless, and in 1952 she left the UK with her children (above). In reality she had known all along that Maclean was a KGB agent and fully supported his defection. In 1953, living in Geneva, she told her mother that she'd be away for the weekend; in reality, she took a train to Austria and was flown to Moscow with her children to join her husband.

On the Bookshelf When You Were Small

The books of our childhood linger long in the memory. These are the children's classics, all published in your first ten years. Do you remember the stories? What about the covers?

1952	Prince Caspian by CS Lewis
1952	**Charlotte's Web by EB White** Charlotte's full name is given as Charlotte A. Cavatica. This is derived from Araneus cavaticus, commonly known as the barn spider.
1952	The Borrowers by Mary Norton
1953	The Silver Chair by CS Lewis
1953	Down with Skool! by Geoffrey Willans
1954	The Eagle of the Ninth by Rosemary Sutcliff
1954	Horton Hears a Who! by Dr Seuss
1956	Kenny's Window by Maurice Sendak
1956	**Hundred and One Dalmatians by Dodie Smith** Dodie Smith wrote the book after one of her friends commented that her dalmatians would make a lovely coat. She had nine - including a Pongo.
1956	The Silver Sword by Ian Serraillier
1956	Little Old Mrs Pepperpot by Alf Prøysen
1957	Moominland Midwinter by Tove Jansson
1957	The Cat in the Hat by Dr Seuss
1958	Five Get into a Fix by Enid Blyton
1958	A Bear Called Paddington by Michael Bond
1958	Tom's Midnight Garden by Philippa Pearce
1959	Silly Verse for Kids by Spike Milligan
1959	The Rescuers by Margery Sharp
1960	**Green Eggs and Ham by Dr Seuss** A $50 bet, laid and won: could Dr Seuss write a book with 50 unique words or fewer? Oh yes, he can!
1960	Tintin in Tibet by Hergé
1960	Weirdstone of Brisingamen by Alan Garner

Around the World in Your Birth Year

Here are the events from abroad that were big enough to make news at home in the year you were born. And you won't remember any of them!

+ Pakistan's first prime minister Liaquat Ali Khan assassinated
+ J D Salinger's seminal novel The Catcher in the Rye published
+ US, Australia and New Zealand sign ANZUS mutual defence pact
+ Shoppers World, one of first US malls, opens in Massachusetts
+ Malaria eradicated in USA
+ US radio DJ Alan Freed coins term 'rock 'n' roll'
+ Marshall Plan ends; $13 billion in US aid given to rebuild Europe
+ Riots in Egypt over UK's refusal to withdraw troops from Suez
+ US 22nd Amendment limits presidents to two terms
+ Geneva opera house catches fire
+ Libya gains independence from Italy
+ Killer Jean Lee last woman to be hanged in Australia
+ First air-dropped nuclear bomb explodes in Nevada desert
+ Fires destroy huge areas of forest in south and west USA
+ Winter of Terror's 650 avalanches kill hundreds in Alpine Europe
+ US couple Rosenbergs guilty of passing atomic secrets to USSR
+ Treaty of Paris establishes European Coal and Steel Community
+ First Pan-American games held in Argentina
+ Sci-fi classic The Day The Earth Stood Still opens in cinemas

Born this year:
- US soul singer Luther Vandross born in New York
- Chess grandmaster Anatoly Karpov born in Zlatoust, Russia
- Sally Ride, first US woman in space, born in Encino, California

Boys' Names When You Were Born

Stuck for a name in the early 20th century? The answer was simple: use your own. Will nobody think of the genealogists? Here are the most popular names in England and Wales in 1951.

John
David
Michael
In America, it's said that 'everyone has an uncle Mike', such is the enduring appeal of Michael as a baby name in the 20th century. But third position in the forties is as good as it got here in the UK.

Peter
Robert
Anthony
Brian
Alan
William
James
Richard
Kenneth
Roger
Keith
Colin
Christopher
Raymond
Rising and falling stars:
Flash in the pan in this Top 100 was Melvyn at 78 (never seen again). Barrie, Reginald, Ernest and Edwin were also heading for the exit, while newcomers included Kevin, Nigel and Terry.

A note about other parts of the UK:
Baby name data isn't available until 1974 for Scotland and the turn of the century for Northern Ireland. How different are they? In the mid-seventies around a third of Scotland's Top 100 boys' names weren't in the English and Welsh equivalent – but the highest ranked of these was Gordon at number 30. By 2019, Scotland-only names ranked 4th (Harris), 7th (Lewis), 18th (Brodie), 22nd (Finlay) and more.

Girls' Names When You Were Born

Some parents pick names that are already popular. Others try to pick something more unusual – only to find out a few years later that thousands had the same idea.

Margaret
Patricia
Christine
Margaret, Christine and Patricia were all at peak popularity but nothing lasts forever: Margaret vanished first, then Patricia, and finally Christine in the mid-eighties.

Mary
Jean
Ann
Susan
Janet
Maureen
Barbara
Valerie
Carol
Sandra
Pauline
Elizabeth
Joan
Pamela
Jennifer
Kathleen
Anne
Sheila
Brenda
Gillian
Linda
Jacqueline
Rising and falling stars:
Blink and you miss it: Glenys and Vivienne were one-hit wonders. But Susan, Carol, Sandra, Linda and Diane would prove they had staying power. Goodbye Beryl, Norma, Cynthia, Mavis and Vera.

Things People Did When You Were Growing Up...

...that hardly anyone does now. Some of these we remember fondly; others are best left in the past!

- ✦ Use a mangle
- ✦ Do your National Service (it ended in 1960)
- ✦ **Use an outside toilet**
  Slum clearances and grants saw the end of most outside toilets, although in 2010 around 40,000 properties still had one.

- ✦ Take the trolley bus to school
- ✦ Fetch coal from the cellar
- ✦ Wear a hat to work
- ✦ **Use a coal tar vaporizer**
  A coal tar inhaler or vaporizer – probably made by Wright's, with the matching liquid – seemed like a good idea for treating whooping cough. It wasn't. A 1930s example held by the National Trust has a simple caption: 'This is poisonous.'

- ✦ Travel without a seatbelt
- ✦ **Rent a TV**
  When tellies cost a fortune (and frequently broke), renting a TV made sense. Where to go? Radio Rentals, who promised, 'You'll be glued to our sets, not stuck with them!'

- ✦ **Wear a housecoat**
  Who can think of a housecoat and curlers without remembering Coronation Street's Hilda Ogden?

- ✦ Scrub your doorstep
- ✦ Creosote the fence (banned for DIY in 2003)
- ✦ **Smoke a pipe**
  Stephen Fry was the last Pipe Smoker of the Year, in 2003.

- ✦ **Spank (or be spanked)**
  Corporal punishment ended in most schools in 1986. It is illegal in Scottish and Welsh homes, but not in England or N. Ireland.

- ✦ Pay the Pools collector
- ✦ Build a soapcart
- ✦ **Write a letter**
  Royal Mail still handles 10 billion letters each year but very few are handwritten. More than a fifth of UK children have never received a letter.

Old-fashioned Games

In a pre-digital age, boardgames ruled. Many of these predate you buy decades, centuries or more but still played; others gather dust in attics and charity shops.

1928	Escalado
1934	Sorry!
1935	**Monopoly** The origins of this stalwart lie with The Landlord's Game, an education tool patented in 1904 by Elizabeth Magie. (The anti-monopoly version – Prosperity – didn't catch on.) It was the first game to feature a never-ending path rather than a fixed start and finish.
1938	Buccaneer
1938	Scrabble
1935	Whot!
1947	Subbuteo
1949	**Cluedo** Cluedo, or Clue as it is known in the USA, introduced us to a host of shady country house characters and a selection of murder weapons. For years those included a piece of genuine lead pipe – thankfully replaced on health grounds.
1925	Dover Patrol
1851	**Happy Families** The original and much-copied Happy Families card game was launched for the Great Exhibition in 1851. For 20th Century children, Happy Families also means the million-selling book series by Allan Ahlberg, based loosely on the card game, which in turn inspired a BBC series.
1889	**Tiddlywinks** Trademarked as Tiddledy-Winks by Joseph Fincher, this much-maligned game has nevertheless found fans at elite universities, spawned countless spin-offs and rule variations (known in Tiddlywink parlance as 'perversions').
1896	Ludo
1892	Chinese Chequers
1938	Totopoly
Ancient Egypt	Mancala

Things People Do Now...

...that were virtually unknown when you were young. How many of these habits are part of your routine or even second nature these days? Do you remember the first time?

+ Shop on Sunday (made possible in England and Wales in 1994)
+ Microwave a curry
+ **Leave a voicemail**
  At least you'll never have to change the cassette again!
+ **Watch last night's TV**
  Nowadays, you don't have to remember to set the VCR (and get a small child to help you do it). BBC iPlayer was the UK's first on-demand, streaming service, launched in 2007.

+ Strim grass
+ Change a fitted sheet
+ Recharge your toothbrush
+ Order a takeaway meal... to be delivered
+ Delete a photo
+ **Fit a disposable nappy**
  The first disposable 'napkins' went on sale in 1949 as two-part Paddis, invented by Valerie Hunter Gordon.

+ Eat an avocado
+ Use Google
+ Take a shower
+ **Make a video call (right)**
+ Buy a cheap flight
+ **Floss your teeth**
  Not a flosser? Take heart from a 2016 US research review: evidence for its benefit is very weak, and official advice to floss was dropped. Poking around with those pesky interdental brushes is how you should be spending your time (and money).

+ Pressure wash your patio
+ **Stick a self-adhesive stamp**
  You can probably still remember the taste of stamp glue, even though the sticky versions were introduced in 1993.

+ Answer an email (or send it to spam)
+ **Use a duvet**
  Sir Terence Conran is credited with finally persuading Brits to ditch the blankets when he introduced duvets in his Habitat stores in the sixties.

Mary Evans / Everett Collection

Zoom, Skype, FaceTime and more: if you weren't making face-to-face calls before the lockdowns of 2020, that's probably when you made your first. But it has taken 50 years to catch on and for technology to catch up: shown above is AT&T's PicturePhone, demonstrated in 1964 at New York's World's Fair. (The cost didn't help: renting a pair of devices for three minutes cost

Popular Food in the 1950s

Few would wish the return of fifties food, even the dishes introduced after rationing finally ended in 1954. Tinned food, stacked high. For flavour, take your pick: ketchup, brown sauce, or salad cream. Keep your olive oil in the bathroom cabinet. But a few favourites live on: who can resist a coronation chicken sandwich?

Milkshakes
Thick, creamy and an ideal hiding place for a lethal dose of poison. That's what the CIA thought when they plotted to slip a pill into Castro's beloved chocolate milkshake. Fortunately for the Cuban leader, the pill stuck to the freezer door.

Chop Suey

Real cream cakes

Bananas
In the 1950s, Gros Michel bananas – the dominant banana sold – were wiped out by the Panama disease, nearly destroying the banana industry.

Peaches

Frosties
Introduced in 1954 as Sugar Frosted Flakes, this new cereal was an instant hit – as was Tony the Tiger.

Frozen chicken

Tinned pineapple
Think pineapple, think Hawaii. Pineapples are still cultivated there, although the state's last cannery closed in 2006.

Spam fritters
Dubbed the 'Miracle Meat' when it was introduced in the late thirties, Spam is no longer made in the UK but it's still popular. Worldwide, around 7 billion cans have been sold; 44,000 cans are still produced every hour.

Baked Alaska

Devilled eggs

Coronation chicken

Hamburgers
In the US during WWII, hamburgers were briefly rebranded 'liberty steaks' in a renewed bout of food-as-propaganda. In World War I, sauerkraut was 'liberty cabbage' while French fries became 'freedom fries' during the Iraq war.

Pre-war Chocolate

Many of the chocolate bars we enjoy today were dreamed up long before WWII – though recipes, sizes and names have mostly been given a tweak or two over the decades to keep them as our newsagent favourites.

1800s	**Fry's Chocolate Cream** The first chocolate bars to be mass-produced.
1905	Cadbury Dairy Milk
1908	Bourneville
1914	Fry's Turkish Delight
1920	Flake
1926	Cadbury's Fruit & Nut
1927	**Jaffa Cake** Her Majesty's Customs and Excise tried to argue that a Jaffa Cake is a biscuit and subject to VAT. McVitie's won the day, in part because Jaffa cakes go hard when stale, unlike biscuits which go soft.
1929	Crunchie
1932	**Mars Bar** Want to buy a Mars bar in the US? Ask for a Milky Way.
1932	Penguin
1935	Aero
1935	**Milky Way** The Milky Way is not named after our galaxy, but instead after a type of malted milk, or milkshake as it's now known.
1936	Milky Bar
1937	**Kit Kat** Before Joseph Rowntree trademarked the term 'Kit Kat' in 1911 and the snack's eventual launch in the thirties, the name was most commonly associated with a mutton pie made by pastry chef Christopher Catt. He served it in his London Kit-Cat Club during the late 17th Century.
1937	Rolo
1939	**Marathon** In 1990, Marathon became Snickers: the US name since its 1930 launch (named after Frank Mars's horse). In the seventies, Mars sold a chocolate bar in the US called the Marathon – and it's still on sale here as the Curly Wurly.

Cars of the 1950s

Do you remember your first road trip? Bare legs welded to the hot plastic seats, buffeted by gusts of warm air through the open windows and not a seatbelt to be seen. There's a fair chance you'll have been cooped up in one of these fifties favourites.

Austin Westminster
Ford Prefect
In The Hitchhiker's Guide to the Galaxy, an arriving alien picks the name Ford Prefect thinking it would be inconspicuous.

Vauxhall Velox
Sunbeam Talbot
Rover 60
Ford Anglia
Features on the cover of Harry Potter and the Chamber of Secrets.

Ford Consul
Hillman Minx
Morris Minor
Originally named Mosquito, the name was changed at the last minute as it was feared that the name would deter conservative buyers. It went on to become the first million-selling British car.

MG Magnette
Morris Oxford
Singer Gazelle
Standard Vanguard
Named after a Navy battleship to appeal to ex-servicemen.

Austin Cambridge
Wolseley / Riley One Point Five
The Riley One Point Five and the Wolseley shared features including the engine, suspension and dimensions. The Riley was originally intended as a replacement for the Morris Minor.

Ford Popular
Land Rover
The first Land Rover was inspired by World War II jeeps, with the steering wheel in the middle. A Land Rover with tank tracks for agricultural work and a monster truck version followed.

Austin A30
Dubbed the steel teddy bear due to its rounded, cute appearance.

1958 brought a rather less welcome motoring innovation: the parking meter. The first meters installed in Mayfair, London (sixpence for an hour, a shilling for two), triggered the predictable result from day one: parked cars crammed onto neighbouring streets without restrictions, below.

The Biggest Hits When You Were 10

Whistled by your father, hummed by your sister or overheard on the radio, these are the hit records as you reached double digits.

Poetry in Motion 🎵 Johnny Tillotson
Are You Lonesome Tonight? 🎵 **Elvis Presley**
This track spent four weeks at the top of the charts and was Presley's seventh UK number one.

Walk Right Back 🎵 The Everly Brothers
Wooden Heart 🎵 Elvis Presley
On the Rebound 🎵 **Floyd Cramer**
On the Rebound was featured in the opening sequence of the 2009 Oscar-nominated movie, An Education.

Surrender 🎵 Elvis Presley
Runaway 🎵 **Del Shannon**
Runaway was the only Del Shannon song to appear on Rolling Stone's list of the 500 Greatest Songs of All Time.

Temptation 🎵 The Everly Brothers
You Don't Know 🎵 Helen Shapiro
Reach for the Stars 🎵 Shirley Bassey
Walkin' Back to Happiness 🎵 **Helen Shapiro**
Helen Shapiro was only 14 when she recorded Walkin' Back to Happiness.

His Latest Flame 🎵 Elvis Presley
Tower of Strength 🎵 Frankie Vaughan
Moon River 🎵 Danny Williams

Tech Breakthroughs Before You Turned 21

Much of the technology we use today stands on the shoulders of the inventions made while you were small. Here are some of the most notable advances.

1951	Wetsuit
1953	Heart-lung machine
1955	Pocket transistor radio
1956	Hard Disk Drive
1956	Operating system (OS)
1957	**Laser** The strength of the first laser was measured in 'Gillettes', as scientists tested the laser by assessing how many Gillette razor blades it could slice.
1958	Microchip
1959	Xerox copier
1959	**Three-point seatbelt** The patented three-point safety belt was first installed by Volvo in 1959. Volvo waived the patent rights so other manufacturers could use the design for free.
1959	Weather satellite
1962	**Red LEDs** It took a further ten years to develop yellow LEDs; blue and white LEDs weren't commercially viable for a further two decades.
1964	Plasma display
1965	Hypertext (http)
1966	Computer RAM
1967	Hand-held calculator
1967	**Computer mouse** Doug Engelbart patented an early version of his 'X-Y indicator' in 1967. By the time a (very large) mouse became available with a Xerox computer in 1981, the patent had expired.
1969	Laser printer
1971	Email

On the Silver Screen When You Were 11

From family favourites to the films you weren't allowed to watch, these are the movies that drew the praise and crowds when you turned 11.

The Day of the Triffids 🎟 Howard Keel, Nicole Maurey
The L-Shaped Room 🎟 Leslie Caron, Anthony Booth
Billy Budd 🎟 Robert Ryan, Peter Ustinov
Dr No 🎟 Sean Connery, Ursula Andress
The iconic first performance of Connery as James Bond.

Jules and Jim 🎟 Jeanna Moreau, Henri Serre
The Music Man 🎟 Robert Preston, Shirley Jones
The Miracle Worker 🎟 Anne Bancroft, Patty Duke
Carry On Cruising 🎟 Sidney James, Kenneth Williams
A Prize of Arms 🎟 Stanley Baker, Helmut Schmid
The Manchurian Candidate 🎟 Frank Sinatra, Angela Lansbury
Walk on the Wild Side 🎟 Laurence Harvey, Jane Fonda
To Kill a Mockingbird 🎟 Gregory Peck, Mary Badham
The American Film Institute voted Atticus Finch as the greatest movie hero of the 20th century.

Cape Fear 🎟 Gregory Peck, Robert Mitchum
Peck punched Mitchum by accident during a fight scene. Mitchum never broke character but collapsed from the impact when he returned to his trailer.

The Longest Day 🎟 John Wayne, Robert Ryan
Mutiny on the Bounty 🎟 Marlon Brando, Trevor Howard
Term of Trial 🎟 Laurence Olivier, Simone Signoret
The Boys 🎟 Richard Todd, Robert Morley
That Touch of Mink 🎟 Cary Grant, Doris Day
Lolita 🎟 James Mason, Sue Lyon
Gypsy 🎟 Rosalind Russell, Natalie Wood
A Kind of Loving 🎟 Alan Bates, June Ritchie
Lawrence of Arabia 🎟 Peter O'Toole, Alec Guinness
O'Toole found the camels so uncomfortable to ride, he used sponge to soften his seat.

Sweet Bird of Youth 🎟 Paul Newman, Geraldine Page
Birdman of Alcatraz 🎟 Burt Lancaster, Karl Malden

Comics When You Were Small

Did you spend your childhood hopping from one foot to the other, longing for the next edition of your favourite comic to appear on the shelves? If so, these may be the titles you were waiting for.

The Hotspur ☀ (1933-1959)
The first-ever issues of the Hotspur were sold with a free black mask. The same mask was rebranded as the Whoopee Mask when it was given away with the Beano debut five years later.

Knockout ☀ (1939-1963)
Knockout Comics (or Knock-Out as they were originally known) ran for 24 years before merging into Valiant. However, the title was revived in 1971 (and the hyphen removed). Unlike most comics of the early 70s, every page was in colour.

Girl ☀ (1951-1964)
Boys Own ☀ (1879-1967)
The Eagle ☀ (1950-1969)
Robin ☀ (1953-1969)
Some of the most popular Robin comic strips included BBC children's characters Andy Pandy and the Flower Pot Men.

TV Comic ☀ (1951-1984)
Tiger ☀ (1954-1985)
The Tiger comic strip character Roy Race was so popular, he eventually became the star of his own eponymous publication in the late 70s – Roy of the Rovers.

The Topper ☀ (1953-1990)
The Beezer ☀ (1956-1993)
For the first 25 years of its run, Beezer – companion to Topper – was printed in large-format A3.

Bunty ☀ (1958-2001)
The Dandy ☀ (1937-2012)
Beano ☀ (1938-present)
The most valuable copies of the first issue of Beano fetch over £17,000 at auction. There are only 20 left in the world today.

Around the UK

10

Double digits at last: you're old enough to eavesdrop on adults and scan the headlines. These may be some of the earliest national news stories you remember.

✦ First edition of The Sunday Telegraph rolls off the presses
✦ Peter Hall founds The Royal Shakespeare Company
✦ Satirical news magazine Private Eye goes on sale
✦ First Mothercare shop opens in Kingston-upon-Thames
✦ Tanganyika (now Tanzania) gains independence from Britain
✦ New act licenses betting shops and bingo halls
✦ British luxury car Jaguar E-type wows crowds at Geneva Motor Show
✦ Britain begins talks to join European Economic Community
✦ Popular religious TV programme Songs of Praise airs on BBC
✦ Birth control pills available on NHS – for married women only!
✦ The Beatles make their debut at Liverpool's Cavern Club
✦ Police Identikit sketch first used to catch criminal
✦ Portland Spy Ring five jailed for passing atomic secrets to USSR
✦ Double agent George Blake tried in secret and jailed for 42 years
✦ Police arrest over 1,300 protestors at London CND rally
✦ Tristan da Cunha islanders evacuated to UK after volcano erupts
✦ Suicide no longer a crime in England and Wales
✦ Farthing ceases to be legal tender
✦ First all-British women's Wimbledon final won by Angela Mortimer
✦ UK's first electronic desktop calculator launched
✦ Rosemarie Frankland becomes first British Miss World

Born this year:
⚹ Princess Diana born Lady Diana Frances Spencer in Norfolk
⚹ World javelin champion Fatima Whitbread born in north London
⚹ Tory MP William Jefferson Hague born in Wentworth, Surrey
⚹ Pop star Boy George born George Alan O'Dowd in Bexley, Kent

UK Buildings

Some were loathed then, loved now; others, the reverse. Some broke new architectural ground, others helped to power a nation or entertain. All of them were built before you were 40.

1951	**Royal Festival Hall** Following the bombing of the Queen's Hall during the Blitz, London was left without a major concert hall. The foundation stone was laid by PM Clement Attlee in 1949.
1961	**Dungeness Lighthouse** When you build a nuclear power station that blocks out the view of a lighthouse, what do you do? Build another one.
1961	**Guildford Cathedral** Scenes from 1976 film The Omen were shot here; cathedral staff had to encourage the locals to attend after filming.
1961	Park Hill, Sheffield
1962	Coventry Cathedral
1964	**Post Office Tower** The tower was previously a designated secret under the Official Secrets Act and didn't appear on any OS maps. It was a pretty prominent secret, though, and was used as a filming location for TV and film during this time.
1966	Birmingham GPO Tower
1966	Centre Point
1966	**Severn Bridge** Grade I listed, and since 2018, free to cross (both ways!).
1967	Queen Elizabeth Hall
1974	**Birmingham Library** Looked like 'a place where books are incinerated, not kept' said Prince Charles. It was demolished in 2013.
1976	National Exhibition Centre (NEC)
1976	**Brent Cross Centre** The UK's first American-style indoor shopping centre. The car park was used for the James Bond film Tomorrow Never Dies.
1980	NatWest Tower
1982	Barbican Centre
1986	Lloyd's Building

Early Radio 1 DJs

Do you remember the first time you heard 'the exciting new sound of Radio 1'? Replacing the BBC Light Programme in 1967, it soon won over the UK's youth to become the world's most popular station, and the DJs – all men until Annie Nightingale joined in 1970 – became household names.

Tony Blackburn
The man who started it all with those immortal words and span the first disc (Flowers in the Rain, by The Move). And don't forget his canine co-presenter, Arnold.

John Peel
Peel's life-long service to music is well known. But before this took off, his aspiration to be a journalist while selling insurance in Texas led him to bluff his way into the midnight news conference where Lee Harvey Oswald was paraded before the press.

Keith Skues

Ed Stewart
For children of the seventies, Ed Stewart means Crackerjack; but for those of us born earlier, it was Junior Choice on Saturday mornings where we'd get to know 'Stewpot'.

Mike Raven

Jimmy Young

Dave Cash

Kenny Everett
Everett was a Radio 1 DJ for less than three years before being sacked. He also appeared in 1980 on Just a Minute and was given the subject of marbles. Nicholas Parsons let him talk (while hesitating, repeating *and* deviating) for 90 seconds as a joke – assisted by the other panellists. He wasn't on the show again.

Terry Wogan

Duncan Johnson

Tommy Vance

Emperor Rosko
'Your groovy host from the West coast, here to clear up your skin and mess up your mind. It'll make you feel good all over!' – Rosko, aka Mike Pasternak, introducing his Midday Spin show.

Pete Murray

Bob Holness

Female Wimbledon Winners

Aged 15 in 1887, Lottie Dod was the youngest to win Wimbledon. Aged 37 in 1908, Charlotte Cooper Sterry was the oldest. These are the winners when you too were still in with a (slim) chance! Men, PTO!

1966-68	**Billie Jean King** King lobbied for equal pay, won the Battle of the Sexes against Bobby Riggs and was the first woman to be chosen as Sports Illustrated's Sportsperson of the Year.
1969	Ann Jones
1970	Margaret Court
1971	Evonne Goolagong
1972-73	**Billie Jean King** King's 1973 Wimbledon marks the last time any player won all three tournaments (singles, doubles, mixed doubles). She didn't win them all in the same day (as Doris Hart did in 1951), but she did manage it twice – she'd scooped the 'triple crown' back in 1967, too.
1974	Chris Evert
1975	Billie Jean King
1976	Chris Evert
1977	**Virginia Wade** Wade competed at Wimbledon 15 times before winning. It was to be Britain's last female grand slam victory until Emma Raducanu's epic US Open win in 2021.
1978-79	Martina Navratilova
1980	Evonne Goolagong Cawley
1981	**Chris Evert Lloyd** Nicknamed the Ice Maiden, Evert was the first tennis player to win 1,000 matches and the first female tennis player to reach $1million in career prize money.
1982-87	Martina Navratilova
1988-89	Steffi Graf

Wimbledon: The Men

In the men's tournament, Becker won at the tender age of 17. At the top end, Federer won in 2017 at the age of 35. But in 1909, in the amateur era, Arthur Gore was a nimble 41 years young – giving us our 'winning window' of 17 to 41.

1968-69	Rod Laver
1970-71	John Newcombe
1972	**Stan Smith**

Outside tennis, Stan Smith is best known for his best-selling line of Adidas sports shoes.

1973	Jan Kodeš
1974	Jimmy Connors
1975	**Arthur Ashe**

Ashe contracted HIV from a blood transfusion following a heart operation, and worked to raise the awareness of HIV and AIDS before his death at the age of 49. The Arthur Ashe Stadium in New York was named in his memory.

1976-80	Björn Borg
1981	John McEnroe
1982	Jimmy Connors
1983-84	John McEnroe
1985-86	**Boris Becker**

As a child, Becker would sometimes practice with Steffi Graf. He dropped out of school to join the West German Tennis Federation.

1987	Pat Cash
1988	Stefan Edberg
1989	Boris Becker
1990	Stefan Edberg
1991	Michael Stich
1992	**Andre Agassi**

Agassi started losing his hair at 19 and wore hairpieces to hide it. The night before the 1990 French Open final, his wig was damaged. He wore it during the match but was so worried about it falling off that he lost.

Books of the Decade

Ten years that took you from kids' adventure books to dense works of profundity – or maybe just grown-up adventures! How many did you read when they were first published?

1961	**Catch-22 by Joseph Heller** The book was originally titled Catch-18 but was changed due to its similarity to the title of the novel Mila 18, which had just been announced.
1961	A House for Mr. Biswas by V S Naipaul
1962	**A Clockwork Orange by Anthony Burgess** Burgess was diagnosed with a brain tumour and wrote five novels in a year to provide his wife with income. It turned out to be a misdiagnosis; he lived for another 30 years.
1962	The Golden Notebook by Doris Lessing
1963	Cat's Cradle by Kurt Vonnegut
1963	V by Thomas Pynchon
1964	Herzog by Saul Bellow
1964	Last Exit to Brooklyn by Hubert Selby
1965	Dune by Frank Herbert
1966	Wide Sargasso Sea by Jean Rhys
1966	The Jewel In The Crown by Paul Scott
1967	One Hundred Years of Solitude by Gabriel Garcia Marquez
1967	The Outsiders by SE Hinton
1967	Poor Cow by Nell Dunn
1968	2001: A Space Odyssey by Arthur C Clarke
1969	Slaughterhouse-Five by Kurt Vonnegut
1969	Portnoy's Complaint by Philip Roth
1969	The Godfather by Mario Puzo
1969	The French Lieutenant's Woman by John Fowles
1969	Them by Joyce Carol Oates
1970	Deliverance by James Dickey

Around the UK

Here's a round-up of the most newsworthy events from across the country in the year you turned (sweet) 16.

+ New town Milton Keynes created in Buckinghamshire
+ BBC Radio 1 and 2 replace the Light Programme
+ Abortion Act legalises terminations on certain grounds
+ BBC2 Wimbledon coverage launches Europe's first colour TV service
+ Kray Twins murder 'Jack The Hat' McVitie
+ Donald Campbell killed in speed record attempt at Coniston Water
+ Government nationalises 90% of British steel industry
+ Act makes it illegal for UK citizens to work for pirate radio
+ Supertanker Torrey Canyon's oil spill turns Cornish seas black (right)
+ Beatles manager Brian Epstein dies of accidental drug overdose
+ BBC's Home Service renamed Radio 4
+ UK's first ATM dispenses cash in Enfield, north London
+ Stockport plane crash kills 72 holidaymakers onboard
+ UK's first local station BBC Radio Leicester launched
+ First North Sea gas pumped ashore at Easington, Yorkshire
+ UK negotiates terms over joining the Common Market
+ North Devon MP Jeremy Thorpe becomes Liberal Party leader
+ Jimi Hendrix sets guitar alight fire on stage at London Astoria
+ Norwell Roberts becomes London's first black police officer
+ Sandie Shaw's Puppet on a String wins Eurovision Song Contest
+ 100-1 outsider Foinavon wins Grand National

Born this year:
- Countdown lexicographer Susie Dent born in Woking, Surrey
- England's first black captain footballer Paul Ince born in Ilford
- Oasis guitarist and songwriter Noel Gallagher born in Manchester
- English footballer Paul 'Gazza' Gascoigne born in Gateshead

Over 100,000 tonnes of crude oil gushed from the Torrey Canyon supertanker when it hit rocks off Land's End in March 1967. A black tide lapped the shores of Brittany; millions of barrels of toxic chemicals were used to 'clean' beaches across Cornwall, causing widespread ecological damage. Bombs, petrol and napalm were dropped to burn off oil and scuttle the ship. It remains the UK's worst ever environmental accident.

TV Newsreaders: The Early Days

Trusted, familiar, and mostly with received pronunciation: these are the faces that brought you and your family the news, and the dates they shuffled their papers.

Richard Baker 📺 (1954-82)
In 1954, Baker introduced the BBC's first TV news broadcast. Seventies children know his voice as the narrator of Mary, Mungo and Midge.

Robert Dougall 📺 (1955-73)
Kenneth Kendall 📺 (1955-69)
Angela Rippon 📺 (1975-2002)
The UK's first regular female newsreader and known nationwide for her 1976 Morecambe and Wise appearance.

Jill Dando 📺 (1988-99)
The shocking murder of Dando on her doorstep in 1999 remains unsolved.

Moira Stuart 📺 (1981-2007)
Peter Woods 📺 (1964-81)
Woods is the biological father of BBC journalist and presenter Justin Webb.

Nan Winton 📺 (1960-61)
Winton was the BBC's first on-screen female newsreader in a shortlived 1960 trial deemed unacceptable by viewers.

Reginald Bosanquet 📺 (1967-79)
Michael Aspel 📺 (1960-68)
Corbet Woodall 📺 (1963-67)
Anna Ford 📺 (1976-2006)
Jan Leeming 📺 (1980-87)
Lynette Lithgow 📺 (1988-96)
Selina Scott 📺 (1980-86)
Sue Lawley 📺 (1981-88)
Alongside her news duties, Lawley is best known for her 18-year stint presenting BBC Four's Desert Island Discs. She left the role in 2006.

Julia Somerville 📺 (1983-99)

Fifties TV Gameshows

Gameshows got off to a rocky start in the UK, but the advent of commercial TV in 1955 – and ad-funded prizes – boosted the format into primetime, where it has remained ever since. Many of these early shows have since been remade, but how many of the originals do you remember?

Tell the Truth

Twenty Questions
Host Gilbert Harding, dubbed by the BBC as Britain's 'best-loved and best-hated man', was particularly drunk during one recording. He insulted two of the panellists, caused chaos by failing to recognise an answer, and ended the show early. Read more about Harding on page 36.

What's My Line?
Arguably the nation's first TV gameshow, first on screens in 1951.

Round Britain Quiz
Top of the Form
Twenty-One
Beat the Clock
Concentration
Crackerjack
Do You Trust Your Wife?

Double Your Money
In 1959, Sir Bobby Charlton appeared as a contestant on the show and won the top prize of £1,000, answering questions on pop music. Dame Maggie Smith also appeared as a hostess for a short time before her acting career took off.

Name That Tune
Opportunity Knocks
Spot the Tune

Take Your Pick!
Take Your Pick! was the first gameshow to be broadcast on commercial TV, debuting on the newly launched ITV in 1955. The income generated by adverts made it the first UK gameshow to give away cash prizes.

Two for the Money
Keep it in the Family
Make Up Your Mind

Stamps When You Were Young

Stamp collecting was the first serious hobby for many 20th century children. Commemorative issues weren't issued until the twenties, but soon became highly collectible – and the perfect gift for uncles in need of inspiration. These stamps may well have started your collection.

1924-5	**British Empire Exhibition** Designed to showcase Britain's strengths in an era of declining global influence, the exhibition left a legacy: the Empire Stadium (later renamed Wembley Stadium). The stamps were the UK's first commemorative issue, sixty years after the USA did the same.
1929	**9th Universal Postal Union Congress, London** Arguably of little interest to few outside philatelic circles, this was the first of several self-referential issues over successive decades. See also the Inter-Parliamentary stamps first issued in 1957.
1935	George V Silver Jubilee
1937	George VI Coronation
1940	**Centenary of the first adhesive postage stamp** Everyone has heard of the first adhesive stamp, issued in 1840: the Penny Black. (Perforations didn't come along until the 1854 Penny Red.) The glue on commemorative stamps contained around 14 calories!
1946	Victory
1948	Royal Silver Wedding
1948	Olympic Games
1949	The 75th Anniversary of the Universal Postal Union
1951	Festival of Britain
1951	George VI (high value 'definitives')
1953	The coronation of Queen Elizabeth II
1955	Castles (high value 'definitives')
1957	**World Scout Jamboree** Held in Sutton Coldfield; 50,000 Scouts attended. After heavy rain, the US Air Force was called in to help.
1957	46th Inter-Parliamentary Union Conference
1958	6th British Empire and Commonwealth Games

The Biggest Hits When You Were 16

The songs that topped the charts when you turned 16 might not be in your top 10 these days, but you'll probably remember them!

I'm a Believer 🎵 The Monkees
This track was written by Neil Diamond, who was working as a songwriter-for-hire. He originally tried to give the song to country singer Eddie Arnold.

This Is My Song 🎵 Petula Clark
Release Me 🎵 Engelbert Humperdinck
Somethin' Stupid 🎵 Nancy and Frank Sinatra
Puppet on a String 🎵 Sandie Shaw
Silence Is Golden 🎵 The Tremeloes
A Whiter Shade of Pale 🎵 Procol Harum
Many people think the lyrics were inspired by the works of Geoffrey Chaucer, but songwriter Keith Reid has admitted that he has never read Chaucer in his life.

All You Need Is Love 🎵 The Beatles
San Francisco 🎵 Scott McKenzie
This song went straight to number one and is considered the anthem of the Summer of Love.

The Last Waltz 🎵 Engelbert Humperdinck
Massachusetts 🎵 Bee Gees
The Bee Gees intended to give this song to the Seekers. When they weren't able to reach them, they decided to record it themselves. They had never been to Massachusetts.

Let the Heartaches Begin 🎵 Long John Baldry
Hello, Goodbye 🎵 The Beatles

Gameshow Hosts of the Fifties and Sixties

Many of these men were semi-permanent fixtures, their voices and catchphrases almost as familiar as our family's. Some were full-time entertainers, born to the stage; others seemed rather less suited to the spotlight!

Ted Ray... ⬦ (Joker's Wild)
and his son, Robin Ray ⬦ (Face the Music)
Peter Wheeler ⬦ (Crossword on Two, Call My Bluff)
Robert Robinson ⬦ (Brain of Britain, Ask the Family)
McDonald Hobley ⬦ (Come Dancing, It's a Knockout)
David Jacobs ⬦ (Juke Box Jury)
Shaw Taylor ⬦ (Password, Pencil and Paper)
Eamonn Andrews ⬦ (Crackerjack!)
Roy Plomley ⬦ (Many a Slip)
Gilbert Harding ⬦ (Twenty Questions, What's My Line?)
Harding was a teacher and policeman before working in radio and television. Resentful of his fame, Harding was once left mortified on the London Underground when he was recognised by fellow passengers who failed to notice that TS Eliot was also in the same carriage.

Bamber Gascoigne ⬦ (University Challenge)
Tommy Trinder ⬦ (Sunday Night at the Palladium)
Bruce Forsyth ⬦ (Beat the Clock)
Bruce Forsyth first appeared on television in 1939. He had many talents including playing the ukulele and accordion, singing, dancing and acting. In his later years, Forsyth stated that he regretted presenting so many gameshows.

Leslie Crowther ⬦ (Billy Cotton Band Show, Crackerjack)
Bob Monkhouse ⬦ (The Golden Shot)
While serving in the RAF, Bob Monkhouse drafted a letter to the BBC from his group captain, stating that 18-year-old Monkhouse was a war hero and deserved an audition. His group captain signed the letter without reading it; Monkhouse got his audition.

Hughie Green ⬦ (Opportunity Knocks)
Derek Batey ⬦ (Mr and Mrs)
Wilfred Pickles ⬦ (radio show Have a Go)

Kitchen Inventions

The 20th-century kitchen was a playground for food scientists and engineers with new labour-saving devices and culinary shortcuts launched every year. Here are some your parents – and now you – wouldn't be without.

1929	**Dishwasher** The first hand-operated dishwasher was created in 1885 by inventor and socialite, Josephine Cochrane, who was tired of her servants chipping her fine china. In 1929, Miele brought out an electric, top-loading model. Front-loading and drying functions followed in 1940; automation in 1960.
1937	Blender
1939	Pressure cooker
1940	Chest freezer
1945	**Fridge** If you think today's American-style fridges are big, consider the Large Hadron Collider in Geneva. With a circumference of 17 miles and 9,300 magnets, it's chilled to -270C before use. That would definitely keep your milk cold.
1948	Kenwood mixer
1955	Automatic kettle
1956	**Non-stick pan** You can thank a French angler's wife for your non-stick pans: it was she who noticed her husband's habit of coating his gear in non-stick Teflon, and suggested he did the same to her pans. Scrambled egg fans owe her a life-long debt.
1960	**Tupperware** In 1960, Tupperware parties arrived in the UK. Earl Tupper's 1948 invention took off when a US single mother called Brownie Wise started home sales and the social selling concept proved equally successful here. This icon of female entrepreneurship was dismissed in 1958 for being too outspoken.
1974	Microwave
1974	Food processor
1976	**Deep fat fryer** The Egyptians, Romans and Greeks were all known to have been keen on deep frying their food – often items that look uncommonly like today's doughnuts (minus the jam).

Around the World When You Turned 18

These are the headlines from around the globe as you were catapulted into adulthood.

- US and Soviet subs K-19 and Gato collide in Barents Sea
- South Africa's most destructive quake hits Western Cape
- Native American rights activists occupy Alcatraz Island
- Yasser Arafat becomes leader of Palestine Liberation Organisation
- US-North Vietnamese peace negotiations fail
- The Beatles play last public gig on Apple Records roof in London
- 500,000 march on Washington in anti-Vietnam War protest
- Republican Richard Nixon sworn in as 37th US president
- US Apollo 11 lands on moon; Neil Armstrong takes first moonwalk
- US senator Ted Kennedy found guilty of Chappaquiddick car crash
- UCLA student sends first internet message: 'LO' (the system crashed)
- Bloodless coup brings Colonel Gaddafi to power in Libya
- British Dickensian musical Oliver! wins six Oscars
- Boeing 747 jumbo jet makes first commercial flight
- 400,000 attend Woodstock music festival on New York farm
- New York Stonewall riots mark start of gay rights movement
- Franco closes border with Gibraltar after it votes to stay in UK
- John Lennon and Yoko Ono bed-in for peace in Amsterdam
- Golda Meir elected as Israel's first woman prime minister

Born this year:
- Spanish actor Javier Bardem born in Las Palmas, Canary Islands
- Oscar-winning actress Cate Blanchett born in Ivanhoe, Australia
- West Indies cricketer Brian Lara born in Santa Cruz, Trinidad
- US rapper Jay Z born Shawn Corey Carter in New York

Toys of Your Childhood

In the sixties, the toy industry got serious: no more lead paint. New licensing models (Thunderbirds! Batman! Doctor Who!). And a Toy of the Year award – the James Bond Aston Martin car was the first winner. Hop into the seventies and you'd soon be needing some batteries to go with some of those Christmas surprises…

Sindy

Katie Kopykat

Betta Bilda

Plasticraft

Peter Powell Stunter

Not to be confused with the popular Radio 1 DJ, Powell was a kite designer who hit the big time after one of his models was featured on the BBC show Nationwide. His revolutionary idea was to use two lines for added control. 'It tugs at the heart strings,' he told the BBC in 2014.

Playmobil

Action Man

Duplo

Spacehopper

Just sneaking into this decade (if Spacehoppers can sneak): these went on sale in 1969. Sold as Hoppity Hops in the USA. In 2018, Steven Payne crossed the Alps on one. Madness.

Ping Pong

Nerf ball

Skateboards

Lego

The world's biggest manufacturer of tyres is not Goodyear, or Michelin – it's Lego. They produce around 300 million tiny tyres every year.

Evel Knievel Stunt Cycle

Etch-a-Sketch

Magna Doodle

Simon

Speak and Spell

The Speak and Spell was the first mass-produced item to include a digital signal processor, a precursor to the computers we have in our homes today.

Around the UK

Voting. Placing a bet. Buying a legal drink. Turning 18 is serious stuff. Here's what everyone was reading about in the year you reached this milestone.

✦ Ocean liner Queen Elizabeth 2 makes maiden voyage to New York
✦ British troops deployed in Northern Ireland in response to riots
✦ Death penalty for murder abolished
✦ Robin Knox-Johnston first to sail solo non-stop around globe
✦ Pre-decimal halfpenny coins phased out
✦ John Lennon weds Japanese artist Yoko Ono in Gibraltar
✦ Aussie media mogul Rupert Murdoch takes over News of the World
✦ Oarsman John Fairfax first to row solo across Atlantic
✦ Victoria Line opens on London Underground
✦ Charles, Prince of Wales, receives title in Caernarfon
✦ John Lennon returns MBE over UK complicity in Vietnam and Biafra
✦ Cult toy Space Hopper bounces into the shops
✦ The Beatles give last public performance on Apple Records roof
✦ Surreal sketch show Monty Python's Flying Circus airs on BBC1
✦ Ulster unionist Rev. Ian Paisley jailed over illegal protest
✦ Kray Twins Reggie and Ronnie sentenced to life for double murder
✦ Concorde makes first test flight at twice the speed of sound (right)
✦ Regular colour TV broadcasts begin on BBC1 and ITV
✦ Gibraltar's border with Spain closed by General Franco
✦ Lionel Bart's Dickensian musical Oliver! wins six Oscars
✦ Quirky kids' series The Clangers first broadcast on BBC1

Born this year:
ൟ 12 Years A Slave director Steve McQueen born in London
ൟ Award-winning actress Catherine Zeta-Jones born in Swansea
ൟ Fashion designer Alexander McQueen born in London

Concorde made its first scheduled flight in 1976, but seven years earlier the first prototypes left the hangar: Concorde 001 (made in France), and Concorde 002, made in Bristol. Chief test pilot Brian Tubshaw (top left) is seen above preparing for its maiden flight on 9 April alongside co-pilot John Cochrane.

Concorde's livery changed several times over its lifetime but was only certified when predominantly white to keep the temperature down at supersonic speeds. There was one exception: in 1996, Pepsi paid to paint one aircraft blue as part of its $500m rebrand. The paint job carried a speed restriction.

Medical Advances Before You Were 21

A girl born in the UK in 1921 had a life expectancy of 59.6 years (boys: 55.6). By 2011 that was up to 82.8 (79 for boys), thanks to medical advances including many of these.

1951	Munchausen syndrome (described)
1952	**Artificial heart** The first artificial heart was built by General Motors. Before the operation, the patient saw two dogs with shaved chests running around, and discovered that they had been the final test subjects. The patient survived the procedure too.
1953	Ultrasound
1956	Paracetamol
1957	EEG topography (toposcope)
1958	Pacemaker
1959	Bone marrow transplant, in-vitro fertilisation
1960	Kidney transplant, CPR and coronary artery bypass surgery
1961	The pill
1962	Hip replacement, beta blockers
1963	**Valium** Valium was famously dubbed 'mother's little helper' by The Rolling Stones. Valium was hailed as a wonder drug as it worked was a far less risky alternative to barbiturates.
1963	Lung transplant, artificial heart
1964	Measles vaccine
1965	**Portable defibrillator** CPR on TV is successful one time in two, a 2009 study found: roughly the same as reality. However, the lack of follow-up or age-related differences on TV means people's expectation for a life-saving result is unrealistically high.
1966	Pancreas transplant
1967	Heart transplant
1968	Liver transplant, Controlled drug delivery
1969	**Cochlear implant** Cochlear implants aren't always a success. Some can't get on with them; others believe they undermine deaf culture.

Popular Girls' Names

20 If you started a family at a young age, these are the names you're most likely to have chosen. And even if you didn't pick them, a lot of British parents did!

Susan
Julie
Karen
Jacqueline
Deborah
Tracey
Tracey, or Tracy? No matter, they're both in vogue (though not for long: they're gone by the eighties).
Jane
Helen
Diane
Sharon
Tracy
Angela
Sarah
Alison
Caroline
Amanda
Sandra
Linda
Catherine
Elizabeth
Carol
Joanne
Wendy
Janet
Dawn
Christine

Rising and falling stars:
Huge changes are afoot here, as for society at large: a third of names make their last appearance including Pamela, Carole, Pauline, Annette and Shirley. Shorter names are in: Kim, Lisa, Sara and more.

41

Animals Extinct in Your Lifetime

Billions of passenger pigeons once flew the US skies.
By 1914, they had been trapped to extinction. Not every
species dies at our hands, but it's a sobering roll-call.
(Date is year last known alive or declared extinct).

1951	Yemen gazelle
1952	**Deepwater cisco fish, USA** The deepwater cisco, once found in two Michigan lakes, was overfished and crowded out by invasive parasites and herring. Result? Extinction.
1952	San Benedicto rock wren, Mexico
1960	Candango mouse, Brasilia
1962	Red-bellied opossum, Argentina
1963	Kākāwahie honeycreeper, Hawaii
1964	South Island snipe, New Zealand
1966	Arabian ostrich
1967	Saint Helena earwig
1967	**Yellow blossom pearly mussel, USA** Habitat loss and pollution proved terminal for this resident of Tennessee.
1968	Mariana fruit bat (Guam)
1971	Lake Pedder earthworm, Tasmania
1972	Bushwren, New Zealand
1977	Siamese flat-barbelled catfish, Thailand
1979	Yunnan Lake newt, China
1981	Southern gastric-brooding frog, Australia
1986	Las Vegas dace
1989	Golden toad (see right)
2000	**Pyrenean ibex, Iberia** For a few minutes in 2003 this species was brought back to life through cloning, but sadly the newborn ibex died.
2001	Caspian tiger, Central Asia
2008	Saudi gazelle
2012	**Pinta giant tortoise** The rarest creature in the world for the latter half of his 100-year life, Lonesome George lived out his days in the Galapagos as the last remaining Pinta tortoise.

The observed history of the golden toad is brief and tragic. It wasn't discovered until 1964, abundant in a pristine area of Costa Rica. By 1989 it had gone, a victim of rising temperatures.

Popular Boys' Names

Here are the top boys' names for this year. In many instances it's merely a reshuffle of the popular names from the previous decade; but in the lower reaches, change is afoot…

David
Paul
Andrew
Mark
John
Michael
Stephen
Ian
Robert
Richard
Christopher
Peter
Simon
Anthony
Kevin
Gary
Steven
Steven stormed the Top 100 in the fifties and reached his peak here at 17. While all around him rose and fell, Steven stayed put for thirty long years.

Martin
James
Philip
Alan
Neil
Nigel
Timothy
Colin
Graham
Rising and falling stars:
Plenty of snappy new entrants here including Sean, Carl, Wayne and Dean. Multisyllabic Jeffrey (and Geoffrey), Vincent, Douglas and Francis enjoyed their last outing.

Popular Movies When You Were 21

The biggest stars in the biggest movies: these are the films the nation was enjoying as you entered adulthood.

Pulp 🎬 Michael Caine, Mickey Rooney
Sleuth 🎬 Laurence Olivier, Michael Caine
Agurrie, Wrath of God 🎬 Klaus Kinski, Ruy Guerra
Last Tango in Paris 🎬 Maria Schneider, Marlon Brando
The Poseidon Adventure 🎬 Gene Hackman, Ernest Borgnine
Frenzy 🎬 Barry Foster, Jon Finch
Deliverance 🎬 Burt Reynolds, Jon Voight
Billy Redden played the banjo player but did not know how to play his instrument. A skilled banjo player hid behind him.
The Amazing Mr Blunden 🎬 Laurence Naismith, Lynne Frederick
Play It Again, Sam 🎬 Woody Allen, Diane Keaton
One of the few Woody Allen movies not shot or set in New York.
Under Milk Wood 🎬 Richard Burton, Elizabeth Taylor
Ooh... You Are Awful 🎬 Dick Emery, Derren Nesbitt
Solaris 🎬 Natalya Bondarchuk, Donatas Banionis
Young Winston 🎬 Simon Ward, Robert Shaw
The Godfather 🎬 Marlon Brando, Al Pacino
Francis Ford Coppola was in danger of being fired from this movie. The studio was unhappy with the product and it wasn't until they saw the scene where Michael kills Sollozzo and McCluskey in the restaurant that they were convinced.

The Candidate 🎬 Robert Redford, Peter Boyle
What's Up, Doc? 🎬 Barbra Streisand, Ryan O'Neal
Everything You Always Wanted to Know About Sex* (But Were Afraid to Ask) 🎬 Woody Allen, Gene Wilder
Mutiny on the Buses 🎬 Reg Varney and Doris Hare
Bless This House 🎬 Sid James, Diana Coupland
Cabaret 🎬 Liza Minnelli, Michael York
Holds the record for the most Oscars (8) without Best Picture.
Sitting Target 🎬 Oliver Reed, Ian McShane
The Ruling Class 🎬 Peter O'Toole, Alastair Sim
Tales from the Crypt 🎬 Joan Collins, Ralph Richardson

Around the UK

A selection of national headlines from the year you turned 21. But how many can you remember?

- ✦ BBC quiz show Mastermind screened for first time
- ✦ IRA car bomb kills seven at Aldershot barracks
- ✦ Duke of Windsor, formerly King Edward VIII, dies in Paris
- ✦ Bloody Sunday – UK troops kill 14 on Derry civil-rights march (right)
- ✦ Second Cod War begins as Iceland declares 50-mile exclusion zone
- ✦ UK far-left group The Angry Brigade go on trial for bombings
- ✦ British direct rule imposed; Northern Irish parliament suspended
- ✦ SAS parachutes into Atlantic to deal with QE2 bomb threat
- ✦ Thousands join CND four-day march to Aldermaston
- ✦ Long-running ITV soap Emmerdale broadcast for first time
- ✦ Luxury electric train Brighton Belle makes last trip from London
- ✦ UK unemployment tops one million
- ✦ School leaving age raised from 15 to 16
- ✦ Staines air crash kills all 118 onboard
- ✦ UK's last UK trolleybus makes final journey in Bradford
- ✦ Coal miners accept pay offer after seven-week strike
- ✦ First official UK Gay Pride rally held in London
- ✦ Deported Ugandan Asians start to arrive in UK
- ✦ Rock opera Jesus Christ Superstar opens in London's West End
- ✦ First official England-Scotland women's football match played
- ✦ Rose Heilbron first female judge to sit at Old Bailey

Born this year:
- ⮞ Ginger Spice Geri Halliwell born in Watford
- ⮞ Olympic gold-medallist rower James Cracknell born in Sutton, Surrey
- ⮞ Actor and DJ Idris Elba born in Hackney, London

Keystone Pictures USA/zumapress.com/Mary Evans

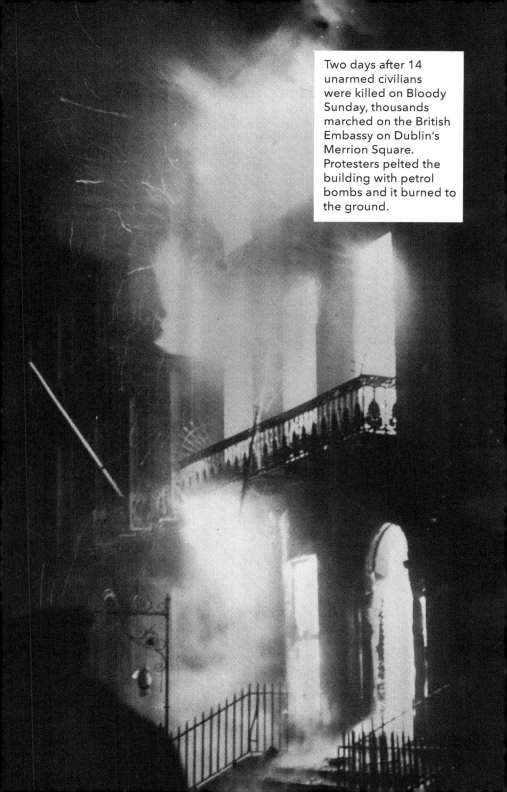

Two days after 14 unarmed civilians were killed on Bloody Sunday, thousands marched on the British Embassy on Dublin's Merrion Square. Protesters pelted the building with petrol bombs and it burned to the ground.

The Biggest Hits When You Were 21

The artists you love at 21 are with you for life. How many of these hits from this milestone year can you still hum or sing in the bath?

Telegram Sam ♪ T Rex
Son of My Father ♪ Chicory Tip
Without You ♪ Nilsson
Amazing Grace ♪ Royal Scots Dragoon Guards
Metal Guru ♪ T Rex
Vincent ♪ Don McLean
Don McLean's timeless classic Vincent was inspired by Vincent Van Gogh's painting, The Starry Night.

Take Me Bak 'Ome ♪ Slade
Puppy Love ♪ Donny Osmond
Donny Osmond featured in a cartoon cameo in the children's television show, Johnny Bravo.

School's Out ♪ Alice Cooper
The album cover for School's Out opens like a school desk (you can see the original in the Hard Rock cafe in Las Vegas). The original vinyl was wrapped in a pair of paper knickers.

You Wear It Well ♪ Rod Stewart
How Can I Be Sure ♪ David Cassidy
Mouldy Old Dough ♪ Lieutenant Pigeon
My Ding-a-Ling ♪ Chuck Berry
Chuck Berry may have helped invent rock'n'roll, but this is the only number one of his entire career.

Popular Food in the 1960s

Convenient ready meals, 'fancy foreign food'... the sixties menu had it all. The chemists joined the dinner party, too, with additives and processes that made our new favourites easy and cheap to produce. We'd take a while to work out if this was always such a good idea!

Vesta curry or Chow Mein

Lager
'Lager' comes from the German word 'lagern', meaning 'to store', as lager takes longer to produce than other ales.

Coco Pops

Fish fingers
The largest fish finger ever made was 6ft long and weighed 136 kg. No word on whether the chef dipped it in ketchup.

Spaghetti Bolognese
You shouldn't include oregano, basil or garlic in the 'ragu' (not bolognese). And for goodness' sake, use tagliatelle, not spaghetti. Or... accept that it is as inauthentic as the Vesta curry and enjoy, like millions of Brits learned to do in the sixties.

Chicken Tikka Masala

Cheese and onion crisps
The first flavoured crisps were created by Joe 'Spud' Murphy (founder of Irish brand Taytos) in the late 1950s.

Crêpe Suzette

Chicken liver pâté

Angel Delight
Angel Delight doubled the dessert market when it was invented in 1967. Wallace and Gromit gave it another push in 1999.

Fray Bentos pies

Instant coffee

Frozen vegetables
Clarence Birdseye was the first person to freeze food for mass production, having got the idea from an Inuit in 1912.

Swedish meatballs

White bread
A new Chorleywood process introduced enzymes and additives and high-speed mixing. The result? Soft, cheap bread that sticks to the roof of your mouth. A nation couldn't get enough of it.

Fashion in the Sixties

As a child, you (generally) wear what you're given. It's only in hindsight, on fading slides, that you recognize that your outfits carried the fashion imprint of the day. Whether you were old or bold enough to carry off a pair of bell bottoms, though, is a secret that between you and your photo albums!

Shift dresses
Mini skirt
Popularised by Mary Quant who named the skirt after her favourite car – although not everyone was a fan. Coco Chanel described the skirt as 'just awful', and it was banned in some European countries.

Five-point cut
Vidal Sassoon
Sassoon had a temper. He would give clients a slap of a comb if they touched their hair while he was cutting it.

John Bates
Biba
Biba started as a mail order business, advertising a pink gingham dress in the Daily Mirror. 17,000 orders were placed and a shop was opened. On its opening day, the store sold out of its only product line.

St Michael American Tan tights
Dr Scholl
Orlon, Crimplene, Terylene, Spandex, PVC and Vinyl
Paper dresses
Twiggy
Jackie Kennedy
In 1962, Jackie Kennedy wore a leopard print coat which caused a spike in demand for leopard skin, leading to the death of up to 250,000 leopards. The coat's designer, Oleg Cassini, felt guilty about it for the rest of his life.

Little black dress
First introduced by Coco Chanel in the 1920s, the little black dress received a fifties update from Christian Dior. Audrey Hepburn's LBD sold for £467,200 in 2006.

Jean Shrimpton
Jane Birkin

Around the World When You Turned 25

By your mid-twenties, TV coverage of news in far-flung places brought global stories into our homes almost as fast as they happened. How many do you remember?

✦ First commercial Concorde flights take off
✦ 7.5 magnitude quake leaves 23,000 dead in Guatemala
✦ Over 40 die in cable-car accident in Cavalese, Italy
✦ Harold Wilson resigns; James Callaghan takes over as UK PM
✦ NASA's Viking 1 spacecraft lands on Mars
✦ Democrat Jimmy Carter beats President Ford to take White House
✦ Gymnast Nadia Comaneci scores perfect 10s at Montreal Olympics
✦ Earthquake razes Tangshan in China, 242,000 thought dead
✦ The Seychelles gains independence from Britain
✦ South African police fire on protesting Soweto schoolchildren
✦ Tragicomedy One Flew Over The Cuckoo's Nest wins five Oscars
✦ Basque nationalist inmates escape jail in Segovia, Spain
✦ First Ebola virus outbreaks occur in West Africa
✦ Steve Jobs, Steve Wozniak and Ron Wayne found Apple Computer Inc
✦ Israeli commando raid frees plane hostages in Entebbe, Uganda
✦ 'Kidnapped' US heiress Patty Hearst jailed for bank robbery
✦ US celebrates 200th anniversary of American independence
✦ The Muppets make first appearance on British TV
✦ US rock band The Eagles releases Hotel California album
✦ Blockbuster boxing film Rocky shot in 28 days for under $1million

Born this year:
❧ US actress Reese Witherspoon born in New Orleans, Louisiana
❧ Golden Globe-winning actor Colin Farrell born in Dublin, Ireland
❧ Striker Ronaldo Luís Nazário de Lima born in Itaguai, Brazil
❧ Canadian actor Ryan Reynolds born in Vancouver

Cars of the 1960s

For every much-loved Hillman Imp or trusted Vauxhall Victor, the sixties boasts a glamorous Aston Martin DB5 or a covetable Jaguar E-type. Has any decade delivered for the motoring public like the sixties?

Mini
Famously featured in the 1969 film The Italian Job, Mini manufacturer BMC didn't want the car used in the film and refused to donate any. However, the director insisted that British cars should be used in a British film and over a dozen were used.

Triumph Herald

Vauxhall Victor
The design of the Vauxhall Victor was based on the style of American cars, which didn't appeal to everyone's taste in 1960s Britain. The car also gained a negative reputation for rusting.

Austin 1100

Sunbeam Tiger

Aston Martin DB5
The Aston Martin DB5 has been described as the most famous car in the world, following its 1964 debut in Goldfinger. In 1968, the car used by James Bond in the film was stripped of the weapons and gadgets and resold as a used car. It was stolen in 1997 and is rumoured to be in the Middle East.

Hillman Hunter

Lotus Elan
The Lotus Elan was designed by Ron Hickman, who subsequently left Lotus and went on to design the Black & Decker Workmate. Early versions of the Elan were also available as a kit that could be assembled by the buyer.

Ford Cortina
The Ford Cortina was launched in 1962 and later proved to be the best-selling car of the 1970s in its Mk3 guise. Designed as a new version of the Ford Consul, the name was changed to Cortina after the Italian ski resort Cortina d'Ampezzo, host to the 1956 Winter Olympics.

Rover 3500

MGB

Vauxhall HA Viva

Books of the Decade

Were you a voracious bookworm in your twenties? Or a more reluctant reader, only drawn by the biggest titles of the day? Here are the new titles that fought for your attention.

1971	An Accidental Man by Iris Murdoch
1971	The Day of the Jackal by Frederick Forsyth
1972	**Watership Down by Richard Adams** Watership Down was the first story Adams ever wrote, at the age of 52, based on tales he told his daughters in the car.
1973	Gravity's Rainbow by Thomas Pynchon
1973	Crash: A Novel by J G Ballard
1974	**Tinker, Tailor, Soldier, Spy by John le Carré** David Cornwell, the man behind the pseudonym John le Carré, drew on his personal experience working for MI5 and MI6. He appeared as an extra in the film of the book.
1974	**Carrie by Stephen King** King's first novel, published when he was 26. He disliked the first draft and threw it in the bin; his wife thankfully found it.
1974	The Bottle Factory Outing by Beryl Bainbridge
1975	Shogun by James Clavell
1975	The Periodic Table by Primo Levi
1976	Interview with the Vampire by Anne Rice
1977	Song of Solomon by Toni Morrison
1977	The Shining by Stephen King
1978	The World According to Garp by John Irving
1978	The Sea, The Sea by Iris Murdoch
1978	Tales of the City by Armistead Maupin
1979	**The Hitchhiker's Guide to the Galaxy by Douglas Adams** If 42 is the meaning of life, what's the meaning of 42? Nothing. Adams said it was simply a random number he chose. There's a message in there somewhere…
1979	A Bend in the River by V S Naipaul
1979	Sophie's Choice by William Styron
1980	A Confederacy of Dunces by John Kennedy Toole
1980	The Name of the Rose by Umberto Eco

Stamps in the Sixties

The UK hit its stride with commemorative stamps in the sixties. There were dry centenary and congress issues, but in 1965 the Postmaster General, Tony Benn, removed the need to include a large monarch portrait. The result? The kind of stamps every young collector would want.

1963	Freedom From Hunger
1963	Lifeboat Conference
1963	Red Cross Centenary Congress
1964	Opening of the Forth Road Bridge
1965	Winston Churchill Commemoration
1965	700th anniversary of Parliament
1965	Centenary of the Salvation Army
1965	**Antiseptic Surgery Centenary** Celebrates the introduction of surgical sterilisation by Joseph Lister.
1965	Commonwealth Arts Festival
1965	25th Anniversary of the Battle of Britain
1965	Opening of the Post Office Tower
1966	Westminster Abbey
1966	Landscapes
1966	**1966 World Cup** Stamps to mark England's role as hosts were hastily reissued in August 1966 with ENGLAND WINNERS added.
1966	British birds
1966	British technology
1966	900th anniversary of the Battle of Hastings
1966	**Christmas** The first UK Christmas stamps. The idea was championed by Tony Benn and the stamps designed by two 6-year-olds – winners of a Blue Peter competition.
1967	British wild flowers
1967	British paintings
1967	British discoveries and inventions
1967	Sir Francis Chichester's solo circumnavigation
1968	British bridges
1969	Concorde's first flight

Sixties TV Gameshows

Gameshows in the sixties were dominated by a few stalwarts, though a few short-lived experimental formats and US adaptions were tried. Without any serious competition, audiences were enormous. How many do you remember watching with your family?

Call My Bluff
Almost every episode from the first eight series of Call My Bluff has been wiped from the BBC archives. There were 263 episodes in series one to eight, and only seven episodes still survive.

Face the Music

Just a Minute

Ask the Family

University Challenge
Several celebrities appeared on University Challenge before they became famous. These include Stephen Fry, David Starkey, Sebastian Faulks, Julian Fellowes, and Miriam Margolyes (who swore when she answered a question incorrectly). University Challenge has a claim to be the longest running TV quiz show, alongside A Question of Sport.

For Love or Money

Mr and Mrs
After watching the Canadian version of Mr and Mrs, Derek Batey was inspired to develop a UK version of the show for Border Television. Batey hosted over 500 episodes, as well as 5,000 on stage after developing a theatrical version.

Play Your Hunch

Take Your Pick

Brain of Britain

Double Your Money
A November 1966 episode drew the nation's highest gameshow audience of nearly 20 million viewers.

Exit! It's the Way-Out Show

Many a Slip

Three Little Words

Crossword on 2

Around the UK

Another decade passes and you're well into adulthood. Were you reading the news, or making it? Here are the national stories that dominated the front pages.

- ✦ Over 100 small tornadoes hit north Wales and England
- ✦ Rebel Labour and Liberal MPs set up Social Democratic Party
- ✦ Yorkshire Ripper Peter Sutcliffe found guilty of killing 13 women
- ✦ UK's Bucks Fizz wins Eurovision with 'Making Your Mind Up'
- ✦ Maze prison hunger strikes end, leaving 10 dead
- ✦ The Times bought by Aussie newspaper mogul Rupert Murdoch
- ✦ Steve Davis wins World Snooker Championship for the first time
- ✦ Racial inequality sparks Brixton riots – 300 hurt, £7.5m damage
- ✦ Futuristic sports car DeLorean assembled in Northern Ireland
- ✦ Fire at Goodge Street tube station – one dead, 16 injured
- ✦ Homebase opens its first DIY store in Croydon
- ✦ Penlee lifeboat and Union Starcrew drown in storm off Cornwall
- ✦ Over 7,000 runners take part in first London Marathon
- ✦ Teenager fires blanks at Queen as she rides to Troop the Colour
- ✦ Prince Charles weds Lady Diana Spencer at St Paul's Cathedral
- ✦ BBC sitcom Only Fools and Horses first seen on our screens
- ✦ British Leyland Longbridge dispute ends with 7,000 laid off
- ✦ First death from AIDS recorded in UK
- ✦ UB40 release single 'One in Ten' about UK unemployment rate
- ✦ Oscar-winner Chariots of Fire released in UK cinemas
- ✦ 250,000 protest against US nuclear bases in UK at CND rally

Born this year:
- ⚬ Super-tall England striker Peter Crouch born in Macclesfield
- ⚬ Golden Globe-winning actor Tom Hiddleston born in London
- ⚬ Princess Anne's daughter equestrian Zara Phillips born in London

Keystone Press Agency/Keystone USA via zumapress.com/Mary Evans

Prince Charles had only met Diana Frances Spencer around a dozen times before he proposed to the 19-year-old earl's daughter in 1981, followed by the wedding in July of that year. A whirlwind, certainly, but romance? The pressure to find a bride of the right standing was mounting after a decade in which he had dated women whatever their eligibility (including Diana's elder sister, and Camilla Parker Bowles). And so, despite his doubts, he proposed. They took a honeymoon in Scotland (above).

The Biggest Hits When You Were 30

How many of these big tunes from the year you turned thirty will still strike a chord decades later?

Imagine ♪ John Lennon
Jealous Guy ♪ Roxy Music
The Roxy Music version of Lennon's Jealous Guy was released after the song became a staple in their set as a tribute to the late musician.

This Ole House ♪ Shakin Stevens
Making Your Mind Up ♪ Bucks Fizz
Stand and Deliver ♪ Adam and the Ants
Being with You ♪ Smokey Robinson
Ghost Town ♪ The Specials
Ghost Town was written as a protest song about the UK's state structure and economic crisis.

Japanese Boy ♪ Aneka
Tainted Love ♪ Soft Cell
Tainted Love was anything but an overnight success. It was first recorded as the B-side to a poor-selling record by US singer Gloria Jones (later a member of T-Rex). A British DJ began to include it in his Northern Soul sets and it grew in popularity. Jones re-recorded it without success; only when Soft Cell covered the song in 1981 did it finally take off.

Prince Charming ♪ Adam and the Ants
Every Little Thing ♪ The Police
Under Pressure ♪ Queen and David Bowie
Don't You Want Me ♪ The Human League

...and the Movies You Saw That Year, Too

From award winners to crowd pleasers, here are the movies that played as your third decade drew to a close.

Outland 🎞 Sean Connery, Frances Sternhagen
Mephisto 🎞 Klaus Maria Brandhauer, Rolf Hoppe
Gregory's Girl 🎞 John Gordon Sinclair, Clare Grogan
Raiders of the Lost Ark 🎞 Harrison Ford, Karen Allen
During the airplane fight scene, the plane ran over Ford's knee and tore the ligaments in his right leg. He wrapped the leg in ice and carried on filming.

Excalibur 🎞 Helen Mirren, Nigel Terry
Escape from New York 🎞 Kurt Russell, Adrienne Barbeau
Pieces of the custom-built city set were repainted and repurposed for Blade Runner the following year.

Clash of the Titans 🎞 Harry Hamlin, Judi Bowker
For Your Eyes Only 🎞 Roger Moore, Carol Bouquet
Sharky's Machine 🎞 Burt Reynolds, Rachel Ward
Dragonslayer 🎞 Caitlin Clarke, Peter MacNicol
Gallipoli 🎞 Mel Gibson, Mark Lee
Scanners 🎞 Stephen Lack, Jennifer O'Neill
Body Heat 🎞 William Hurt, Kathleen Turner
Reds 🎞 Warren Beatty, Diane Keaton
The Great Muppet Caper 🎞 Jim Henson, Frank Oz
The Cannonball Run 🎞 Burt Reynolds, Dom DeLuise
An American Werewolf in London 🎞 David Naughton, Jenny Agutter
Blow Out 🎞 John Travolta, Nancy Allen
Condorman 🎞 Michael Crawford, Barbara Carrera
Arthur 🎞 Dudley Moore, Liza Minnelli
Chariots of Fire 🎞 Ben Cross, Ian Charleson
In the true story, it was Lord Burghley (Lindsay in the film) who completed the Great Court Run first, not Harold Abrahams. The real Abrahams did not even compete.

Time Bandits 🎞 John Cleese, Sean Connery
Quartet 🎞 Maggie Smith, Isabelle Adjani
On Golden Pond 🎞 Henry Fonda, Katharine Hepburn

Around the House

Sometimes with a fanfare but often by stealth, inventions and innovations transformed the 20th-century household. Here's what arrived between the ages of 10 and 30.

1961	Cordless power drills
1962	**Satellite television** Despite being invented in 1962, satellite television did not reach the UK until 1990 with Sky, soon to become BSkyB.
1963	Push button telephones
1963	Lava lamps
1964	Flat screen and Portable TVs
1965	**AstroTurf** AstroTurf was originally called ChemGrass, and invented by chemicals giant Monsanto. It was rebranded in 1966.
1965	Cordless phones
1965	Plastic chairs
1967	Ariel detergent
1968	Plastic wheelie bins
1969	Bean bags
1969	Comfort fabric softener
1970	**Blu-Tack** The largest Blu-Tack sculpture is a 2007 creation called Spider Biggus. it uses 4,000 packs of the blue stuff.
1971	Garden strimmers
1973	BIC lighter
1974	Sticky notes
1975	Betamax movies
1976	**VHS movies** The last film ever released on VHS was David Cronenberg's 2006 thriller, A History of Violence.
1977	Sony Walkman
1977	Auto focus cameras
1978	Electronic (computer-controlled) sewing machines
1978	Slide Away (sofa) beds
1979	**Black + Decker DustBuster** Black + Decker came up with the idea of a cordless vacuum while working on a cordless drill for NASA.

British Prime Ministers in Your Lifetime

These are the occupants of 10 Downing Street, London, during your lifetime, not including Larry the resident cat. Don't be deceived by that unassuming, black, blast-proof door: Number 10 features a warren of more than 100 rooms.

1945–51	Clement Attlee
1951–55	Sir Winston Churchill
1955–57	Sir Anthony Eden
1957–63	**Harold Macmillan**

Macmillan was the scion of a wealthy publishing family, but the biggest secret of his life was kept under wraps: his wife Dorothy's 30-year affair with fellow Conservative (and Krays associate) Robert Boothby. Macmillan died aged 92; his last words were, 'I think I will go to sleep now.'

1963–64	Sir Alec Douglas-Home
1964–70	Harold Wilson
1970–74	Edward Heath
1974–76	Harold Wilson
1976–79	James Callaghan
1979–90	**Margaret Thatcher**

'Today we were unlucky,' said the chilling statement from the IRA, 'but remember we only have to be lucky once.' The 1994 bombing of the Grand hotel in Brighton may not have killed the prime minister, but five others died and others were left with lifelong injuries.

1990–97	John Major
1997–2007	Tony Blair
2007–10	Gordon Brown
2010–16	David Cameron
2016–19	**Theresa May**

Asked in a pre-election interview about the naughtiest thing she'd ever done, May said that she'd once run through a field of wheat with her friends, and that the farmers 'weren't too happy'.

2019–	Boris Johnson

Household Goods in 1962

In 1947, the government calculated inflation for the first time using a basket of frequently purchased goods. This list has been reviewed ever since; the changes mirror our ever-changing tastes and habits. Here's what housewives were buying when you were small.

Sliced white bread
Chocolate coated biscuits
Dry cleaning
Potato crisps
Crisps entered the basket of goods in 1962, the same year Golden Wonder (bought by Imperial Tobacco) launched cheese and onion flavoured crisps. Golden Wonder, Smith's and soon Walkers fought for the market, and consumption rocketed.

Oven ready chicken
Cuts of halibut
Second-hand car
Welfare milk scheme
Ground coffee
Frozen croquettes
As more homes had freezers and the desire for ready meals increased, frozen food was all the rage. Frozen croquettes were released in the early 1960s and were a resounding success.

Canned fruit salad
Canned fruit salad was designed to use the fruit scraps that couldn't be used in canning. Fruit salad arrived in the 1940s and became one of the most popular canned fruits available. You could even use it to make a fruit salad cake.

TV set rental
Gloss paint
Ceiling paper
Jeans
Latex backed carpet
Refrigerator
Ready-made suit
Terylene slacks
Created in Manchester in 1941, Terylene revolutionised clothing in the 1950s. It was used by Mary Quant to make the original miniskirts, and Ray Davies of The Kinks advertised it.

Around the World When You Turned 35

It's a big news day every day, somewhere in the world. Here are the stories that the media thought you'd want to read in the year of your 35th birthday.

✦ First virus affecting Windows-based PCs released ('Brain')
✦ Seven crew die as US space shuttle Challenger explodes on lift-off
✦ Computer animation studio Pixar founded in Richmond, California
✦ USSR launches first long-term manned space station Mir
✦ Bangladesh river ferry Shamia capsizes – 600 drown
✦ Hands Across America human chain raises funds for charity
✦ Gorbachev's Glasnost policy aims to open up Soviet politics
✦ Diego Maradona's Hand of God goal helps Argentina win World Cup
✦ Scandal as US funds Nicaraguan Contras from arm sales to Iran
✦ Swedish prime minister Olof Palme shot dead in Stockholm street
✦ Despite 11 nominations The Color Purple wins no Oscars
✦ Bangladesh hit by 1kg hailstones, heaviest ever recorded
✦ Lethal gas from volcanic lake kills 1,200 in Cameroon
✦ Chernobyl reactor blast releases radioactive matter across Europe
✦ South African cleric Desmond Tutu elected Bishop of Cape Town
✦ Halley's Comet visible from Earth for second time this century
✦ US launches Libyan air strikes in response to terrorist attacks
✦ Islamic terrorists kidnap UK journalist John McCarthy in Lebanon
✦ Marcos ousted; Cory Aquino is Philippines' first female president
✦ Outbreak of Mad Cow Disease affects UK livestock

Born this year:
⚘ Spanish tennis ace Rafael Nadal born in Manacor, Mallorca
⚘ Paralympian Oscar Pistorius born in Johannesburg, South Africa
⚘ US pop icon Lady Gaga born Stefani Germanotta in New York
⚘ Super-sprinter Usain Bolt born in Sherwood Content, Jamaica

Beer of the Seventies

You could haul a seven-pint tin of Watneys Party Seven to a celebration. Someone would be drinking bland Watneys Red, or Courage Tavern ('It's what your right arm's for'). But how about a drop of that cold, refreshing lager you tried on holiday? 'Mine's a pint!' said millions of Brits.

Watneys Party Seven

Whitbread Tankard

Watneys Red

Double Diamond

Carlsberg

The inventor of Carlsberg, JC Jacobsen, gave a Ted Talk on his life philosophy in 2017 – 130 years after he died. He was brought back to life via hologram and even fielded questions from the audience.

Heineken

The Heineken International company owns more than 250 other brands, many of which you'll probably recognise such as Amstel, Desperados and Strongbow.

Tennant's Gold Label

Guinness

When Arthur Guinness started his now-famous business he rented an unused brewery on a 9,000-year lease – though the contract was eventually voided when the company bought the land and surrounding areas to expand the business.

Worthington E

Carling Black Label

Harp

Stella Artois

Ind Coope Super

Younger's Scotch Ale

Bass Charrington

Strongbow

HP Bulmer named his drink after one of the greatest knights in English history, Richard de Clare, who was given the nickname Strongbow.

Long Life

Seventies TV Gameshows

With light entertainment increasingly becoming the bedrock of TV channel success, the seventies saw an explosion of formats from gimmicks to US imports. Which ones got you shouting at the telly?

It's a Knockout
Although this show began in 1966 and it limped on into the new century, the seventies was It's a Knockout's golden age, thanks in no small part to presenter Stuart Hall. The winning teams proceeded to represent the UK at the European final, Jeux Sans Frontières.

I'm Sorry I Haven't a Clue
Jokers Wild
My Music

A Question of Sport
A Question of Sport is the world's longest running TV sports quiz. The first episode was recorded in 1970 in a converted chapel in Rusholme, Manchester, and the show is still recorded in the city as it surpasses 1,300 episodes.

Quote... Unquote
Whodunnit?
Mastermind
Screen Test

Celebrity Squares
Inspired by the game noughts and crosses, Celebrity Squares was based on the US gameshow Hollywood Squares. The original run was presented by Bob Monkhouse, who also returned to host the revival of the show in the 1990s.

Gambit
The Generation Game
The Golden Shot
The Indoor League
Password
Runaround
Sale of the Century
The Sky's the Limit
Winner Takes All

Popular Boys' Names

40 Just as middle age crept up unnoticed, so the most popular names also evolved. The traditional choices – possibly including yours – were fast losing their appeal to new parents.

Christopher
Christopher takes a ten-year stint at the top, replacing Paul but ultimately unable to keep Thomas at bay.

James
David
Daniel
Michael
Matthew
Andrew
Richard
Paul
Mark
Thomas
Adam
Robert
John
Lee
Benjamin
Steven
Jonathan
Craig
Stephen
Simon
Nicholas
Peter
Anthony
Alexander
Gary
Ian

Rising and falling stars:
The rapid turnover in fashion hasn't abated: again, a third of names in this list won't be seen again, from Barry to Brian, Antony to Abdul.

Popular Girls' Names

40 It's a similar story for girls' names. Increasing numbers took their infant inspiration from popular culture. The worlds of music, film and now the internet are all fertile hunting grounds for those in need of inspiration.

Sarah
Laura
Gemma
Never seen in the Top 100 before, here's Gemma riding high as the third most popular name in the UK.

Emma
Rebecca
Claire
Victoria
Samantha
Rachel
Amy
Jennifer
Nicola
Katie
Lisa
Kelly
Natalie
Louise
Michelle
Hayley
Hannah
Helen
Charlotte
Joanne
Lucy
Elizabeth
Leanne
Danielle

Rising and falling stars:
This Top 100 list spans much of the eighties and sees a one-off appearance of Charlene. In not-unrelated news, nearly 20 million people watched Jason marry Kylie on Neighbours...

F1 Champions

If you fancy your chances in Formula One, start young. Sebastian Vettel won at 23. *El Maestro*, Juan Manuel Fangio, is the oldest winner to date, at 46. The field is wide open for an older champ, right?

Emerson Fittipaldi 🏁 (1972,74)
Niki Lauda 🏁 (1975,77,84)
Niki Lauda was also an aviation entrepreneur, founding three airlines in Austria. He also held a commercial pilot's licence.

James Hunt 🏁 (1976)
Mario Andretti 🏁 (1978)
Jody Scheckter 🏁 (1979)
Alan Jones 🏁 (1980)
Nelson Piquet 🏁 (1981,83,87)
Nelson Piquet lost his civilian driving licence in 2007 due to numerous speeding and parking offences. He was ordered to attend a week of lessons and pass an exam.

Keke Rosberg 🏁 (1982)
Alain Prost 🏁 (1985-6,89,93)
Ayrton Senna 🏁 (1988,90-1)
Two days before Senna's fatal crash at Imola, he was early to the scene of a near-fatal crash for Rubens Barrichello. One day before, he inspected the car of Roland Ratzenberger as the mortally-injured Austrian was taken to hospital – the same facility that would attempt to save Senna's life the following day after his crash on the same corner. An Austrian flag was later found in Senna's cockpit, intended to be unfurled as a tribute to Ratzenberger.

Nigel Mansell 🏁 (1992)
Michael Schumacher 🏁 (1994-5,2000-04)
Michael Schumacher was one of a handful of drivers to appear as themselves in the Pixar film Cars, voicing a Ferrari F430.

Damon Hill 🏁 (1996)
Jacques Villeneuve 🏁 (1997)

Fashion in the Seventies

The decade that taste forgot? Or a kickback against the sixties and an explosion of individuality? Skirts got shorter (and longer). Block colours and peasant chic vied with sequins and disco glamour. How many of your seventies outfits would you still wear today?

Flares
Platform shoes
Laura Ashley
While working as a secretary, Laura Ashley was inspired to produce printed fabric after seeing a display at the Victoria and Albert Museum. Struggling to make a profit, Laura Ashley and her husband and children once lived in tents in Wales for six months.

Gucci
Diane Von Furstenberg
Tie Dye
Kaftans
Brought to western culture via the hippie trail, the kaftan's popularity was boosted further when Elizabeth Taylor wore a kaftan-inspired dress for her second wedding to Richard Burton in 1975.

Liza Minnelli
Lurex and suede
David Bowie
Afro, braids or a perm
Jumpsuit
Sequin hot pants
Moon boots
Double denim
Double denim garnered the nickname the 'Canadian tuxedo' after Bing Crosby was refused entry to a hotel in Vancouver because he wore a denim ensemble. Levi subsequently designed Crosby a denim tuxedo.

Vivienne Westwood
Previously a primary school teacher, Vivienne Westwood lived in an ex-council flat in Clapham until 2000. Her son from her relationship with Malcolm McLaren founded lingerie brand Agent Provocateur.

Household Goods in 1970

Frozen foods and eating out swallow up an increasingly larger share of the family budget in the seventies. Or how about a day trip (don't forget your AA membership and your mac), then home for a sweet sherry?

Frozen chicken
Mushrooms
Frozen beans
Sherry
Sherry consumption peaked in the UK in the 1970s following the development of sweet versions – often using added syrups or sugars – known as creams and developed for British palates.

Night storage heater
Plastic Mackintosh
MOT test
Introduced in 1960, the MOT was designed to test the brakes, lights, and steering of all vehicles over 10 years old. This was progressively reduced to every three years by 1967, and the test changed to include tyres.

State school meal
Canteen meal
Cup of tea
The 1970s saw a significant increase in eating out, so a cup of tea was added to the basket. Despite Britain's reputation as tea lovers, coffee sales overtook tea sales for the first time in 1986.

Cafe sandwich
Local authority rent
Local authority rent was added to the basket of goods in the 1970s; by 1979, 42% of Britons lived in council homes.

Paper handkerchiefs
Auto association subs
Keg of ale
Fresh cream
Gammon
While gammon gained popularity during the 1970s due to its unlikely pairing with pineapple rings, the word 'gammon' is now also used as an insult towards the political right, coined in response to 'snowflake'.

Post-war Chocolate

You'll find nearly all of these on the supermarket shelves, even though the most recently invented chocolate bar here was brought to market thirty years ago. Gulp.

1948	Fudge
1951	**Bounty** If you wanted to sell a chocolate bar with curved ends and swirls on the top, in theory there's nothing that maker Mars could do to stop you: the shape was decreed not distinctive enough to trademark in 2009. Do check with a lawyer first, though.
1957	Munchies
1958	Picnic
1962	**After Eight Mint Chocolate Thins** A billion of these are churned out every year (although we've never heard anyone call them chocolate thins).
1962	Topic
1963	Toffee Crisp
1967	Twix
1970	Chomp
1970	Curly Wurly
1973	Freddo
1976	**Double Decker** Double Deckers contain raisins, don't they? Not any more: they were removed from the recipe during the eighties.
1976	Starbar
1976	**Yorkie** 'It's not for girls,' said the adverts. The sexist marketing of Yorkie reached its peak – or trough – in 2005 with special pink editions. By 2011 the complaints outweighed the commercial advantage. The 'men only' angle was dropped.
1978	Lion Bar
1980	Drifter
1983	**Wispa** For twenty years, Wispa was the go-to Aero alternative. But then in 2003 it was gone. A predictable outcry followed and in 2007 it was back on the shelves. Phew.
1992	Time Out

Books of the Decade

Family, friends, TV, and more: there are as many midlife distractions as there are books on the shelf. Did you get drawn in by these bestsellers, all published in your thirties?

1981	Midnight's Children by Salman Rushdie
1982	The Color Purple by Alice Walker
1982	**Schindler's Ark by Thomas Keneally**

Keneally wrote Schindler's Ark – later retitled Schindler's List – after he met Holocaust survivor Leopold Page. Schindler is credited with saving over 1,000 lives. He is the only former Nazi to be buried on Jerusalem's Mount Zion.

1983	The Colour of Magic by Terry Pratchett
1983	Waterland by Graham Swift
1984	Money by Martin Amis
1984	Neuromancer by William Gibson
1984	The Wasp Factory by Iain Banks
1985	**The Handmaid's Tale by Margaret Atwood**

The Communist reign of Nicolae Ceaușescu in Romania partially inspired Atwood to write The Handmaid's Tale. While he was in power, women had to have four babies; abortions were illegal, contraception was banned, and women were examined for signs of pregnancy at work.

1985	Blood Meridian by Cormac McCarthy
1985	Perfume by Patrick Suskind
1986	The Old Devils by Kingsley Amis
1986	It by Stephen King
1987	Beloved by Toni Morrison
1987	Bonfire of the Vanities by Tom Wolfe
1988	Satanic Verses by Salman Rushdie
1988	The Alchemist by Paulo Coelho
1988	Oscar and Lucinda by Peter Carey
1988	The Swimming-Pool Library by Alan Hollinghurst
1989	A Prayer for Owen Meany by John Irving
1989	The Remains of the Day by Kazuo Ishiguro
1990	Possession by AS Byatt
1990	The Buddha of Suburbia by Hanif Kureishi

Around the World When You Turned 40

Which of these international news events were on your radar as you clocked up four decades on the planet?

✦ Soviet Union dissolved, replaced by 15 independent republics
✦ Cholera outbreak in Peru kills over 3,000
✦ 138,000 killed by tropical cyclone in Bangladesh
✦ Operation Solomon airlifts Ethiopian Jews to new life in Israel
✦ Milwaukee police catch US 'cannibal' killer Jeffrey Dahmer
✦ Neolithic mummy Ötzi the Iceman found in Italian Alps
✦ Myanmar opposition leader Aung San Suu Kyi wins
     Nobel Peace prize
✦ Former Indian leader Rajiv Gandhi killed by suicide bomber
✦ Black US motorist Rodney King beaten by Los Angeles police
✦ Aussie media mogul Robert Maxwell drowns, leaving empire in ruins
✦ First Sumo match outside of Japan takes place in London
✦ Art worth $500m stolen from Van Gogh Museum, Amsterdam
✦ Japanese firm Sega releases first Sonic the Hedgehog game
✦ Dances with Wolves starring Kevin Costner wins Best Picture Oscar
✦ Boris Yeltsin elected first president of Russian Federation
✦ President Bush declares Iraq ceasefire and Gulf War win
✦ US-led air attack on Iraq Operation Desert Storm begins
✦ Winnie Mandela jailed for kidnapping four youths in South Africa

Born this year:
&ᵖ US actress Shailene Woodley born in San Bernadino, California
&ᵖ Romanian tennis player Simona Halep born in Constanta
&ᵖ Real Madrid player Eden Hazard born in La Louvière, Belgium

The Biggest Hits When You Were 40

Big tunes for a big birthday: how many of them enticed your middle-aged party guests onto the dance floor?

Innuendo ♪ Queen
Innuendo was the title track of the final Queen album with lead singer Freddie Mercury, recorded and released as his health declined.

Do the Bartman ♪ The Simpsons
The Stonk ♪ Hale and Pace
The One and Only ♪ Chesney Hawkes
The Shoop Shoop Song ♪ Cher
I Wanna Sex You Up ♪ Color Me Badd
Any Dream Will Do ♪ Jason Donovan
Primary school favourite Any Dream Will Do hit number one after being recorded by Donovan who was playing the lead role in Joseph at the time.

(Everything I do) I Do It for You ♪ Bryan Adams
Sixteen weeks. That's how long we enjoyed (or endured) Bryan Adams and producer Mutt Lange's massive hit at number one, one of the best-selling songs of all time. It was written in under an hour.

The Fly ♪ U2
Dizzy ♪ Vic Reeves and
The Wonder Stuff
Black or White ♪ Michael Jackson
Home Alone star Macaulay Culkin appeared in the Black of White music video as the young boy who plays the guitar so loud that he shoots his father into outer space.

Bohemian Rhapsody ♪ Queen

Popular Food in the 1970s

Roll out the hostess trolley, seventies food is ready to be served. If it's not highly processed, artificially coloured, moulded and served in a novelty dish, is it even food? Still, most of it went down very well with the kids – and still does today, given half a chance.

Lemon meringue pie

Cheese and pineapple

Black Forest Gâteau

The Black Forest Gâteau is named after the kirsch alcohol made from Black Forest sour cherries, rather than the Black Forest region in Germany.

Dream Topping

Mateus Rose, Liebfraumilch and Chianti

Cornetto

Cornetto cones were created by Spica, an Italian ice-cream company, in 1976. The company was bought by Unilever not long after, who then marketed the dessert in Europe.

Quavers

Quiche

Unlike the gâteau above, quiche Lorraine *was* named after the area in which it was created. It is considered a French dish, even though Lorraine was under German rule at the time.

Pot Noodle

The original Pot Noodle made in 1979 did not contain a sauce sachet – these were only added in 1992.

Fondue

Smash

Scampi in a basket

Banoffee pie

Chili con carne

Chili is the state dish of Texas, where many people think the recipe originated. Before WWII, hundreds of individual parlours all insisted they had their own secret recipe.

Prawn cocktails

Profiteroles

The Full English Breakfast

Cars of the 1970s

How did you get around in the seventies? Was it in one of the decade's fancy new Range Rovers, or perhaps something more modest like a Morris Marina? Here are the decade's most famous (and infamous) cars.

Ford Capri

Vauxhall HC Viva

Ford Escort
Introduced in 1968, the Ford Escort went on to be the best-selling car in Britain in the 1980s and 1990s. The car was brought back into the spotlight in 2013, when it was featured in Fast & Furious 6.

Jaguar XJ

Triumph TR7

Austin Allegro

Austin Maxi
The Austin Maxi was the first British five-door hatchback, and one of the first cars to be featured on the BBC's Wheelbase show.

Ford Cortina

Ford Granada
Designed as a European executive car, the Granada was popular for taxi and police car use. It was also modified for use as a hearse and limousine, and was often seen in The Sweeney.

Leyland Princess

Triumph Dolomite

Vauxhall Cavalier

Range Rover

Morris Marina
The popular Morris Marina is ranked amongst the worst cars ever built. The car was released with poor suspension, chronic understeer, and windscreen wipers fitted the wrong way round.

Hillman Avenger

Saab 99

Datsun Sunny

BMW 316

Volkswagen Beetle
Affectionately known as the bug in English-speaking countries, it is called turtle in Bolivia, frog in Indonesia, and hunchback in Poland.

Household Goods in 1980

Mortgage interest rates were around 15% as we went into the eighties, not much lower as we left, and added to our basket in 1980. If you had any money left over perhaps you were spending it on home perms, cement and lamb's liver!

Lamb's liver

Tea bags
Tea is one of the few items included in the basket since the start. Tea bags were added in 1980; loose tea was removed in 2002.

Smash
Smash sales soared following the 1974 TV adverts featuring the Smash Martians. It was replaced in 1987 by oven chips.

Cider

Wine

Mortgage Interest

White spirit

Cement

Toilet seat

Electric plug

Colour TV
Colour TV sets outnumbered black and white sets in 1976.

Record player

Cassette recorder
Cassette recorders were first introduced by Philips in the 1960s and were originally intended for dictation and journalists.

Electric hairdryer

Carpet sweeper

Continental quilt

Drycell batteries

Colour photo film

Briefcase

Home perm

National Trust fees
Membership to the National Trust significantly increased throughout the 1980s (around 5.6 million people are members today). The Giant's Causeway is the most visited national attraction.

Olympic Medallists in Your Life

With seven gold medals, Jason Kenny is without equal while the unique achievements of Laura Trott – now Mrs Kenny – brings the household tally to twelve. Meanwhile, over at the Paralympics, swimmer-cyclist Sarah Storey has an incredible 17 gold medals. And medals of all colours? Here are the heroes of Team GB at the Summer Olympics.

Jason Kenny (9) 🥇 Cycling
Bradley Wiggins (8) 🥇 Cycling
Britain's most decorated Olympian until Kenny took the crown in Tokyo, Wiggo acquired various nicknames throughout his career. In France he was referred to as 'Le Gentleman', while the Dutch apparently called him 'The Banana with the Sideburns'.

Chris Hoy (7) 🥇 Cycling
Laura Kenny (6) 🥇 Cycling
Our most successful female Olympian with five gold medals, Trott (now Kenny) began life with a collapsed lung and asthma.

Steve Redgrave (6) 🥇 Rowing
Max Whitlock (6) 🥇 Gymnastics
Charlotte Dujardin (6) 🥇 Equestrianism
Ben Ainslie (5) 🥇 Sailing
Known for his hot temper, Ben Ainslie has accused competitors of teaming up against him. He was disqualified from the world championships in Australia for confronting a photographer who Ainslie felt had impeded his progress.

Adam Peaty (5) 🥇 Swimming
Katherine Grainger (5) 🥇 Rowing
Grainger is the first British woman to win medals at five successive Olympic games, from Sydney to Rio.

Mo Farah (4) 🥇 Athletics
Matthew Pinsent (4) 🥇 Rowing
Ed Clancy (4) 🥇 Cycling
Ian Stark (4) 🥇 Equestrianism
Louis Smith (4) 🥇 Gymnastics
Becky Adlington (4) 🥇 Swimming
Seb Coe (4) 🥇 Athletics
Ginny Leng (4) 🥇 Equestrianism

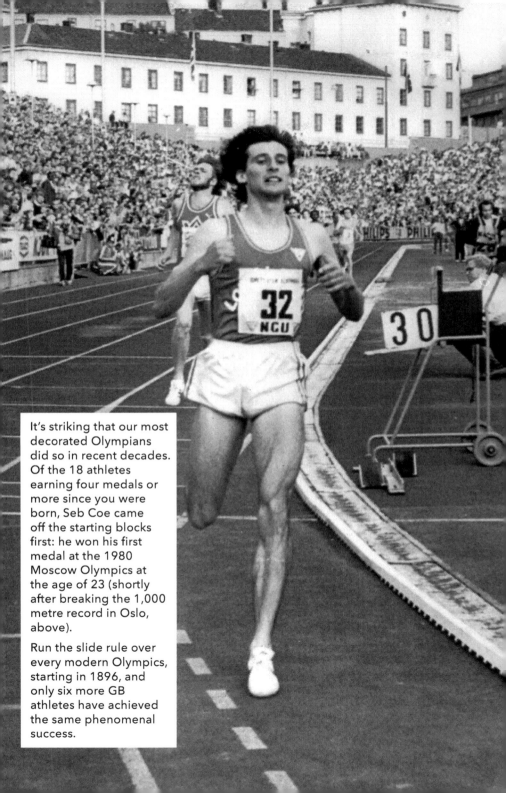

It's striking that our most decorated Olympians did so in recent decades. Of the 18 athletes earning four medals or more since you were born, Seb Coe came off the starting blocks first: he won his first medal at the 1980 Moscow Olympics at the age of 23 (shortly after breaking the 1,000 metre record in Oslo, above).

Run the slide rule over every modern Olympics, starting in 1896, and only six more GB athletes have achieved the same phenomenal success.

Winter Olympics Venues Since You Were Born

Unless you're an athlete or winter sports fan, the Winter Olympics can slip past almost unnoticed. These are the venues; can you remember the host countries and years?

Lillehammer
Cortina d'Ampezzo
Oslo
Salt Lake City
Sapporo
Albertville
The last Games to be held in the same year as the Summer Olympics, with the next Winter Olympics held two years later.

Turin
Grenoble
Beijing
Sarajevo
Lake Placid
Sochi
Innsbruck (twice)
This usually snowy city experienced its mildest winter in 60 years; the army was called in to transport snow and ice from the mountains. Nevertheless, twelve years later, the Winter Olympics were back.

Squaw Valley
Nagano
Calgary
Vancouver
PyeongChang

Answers: Lillehammer: Norway, 1994; Cortina d'Ampezzo: Italy, 1956; Oslo: Norway, 1952; Salt Lake City: USA, 2002; Sapporo: Japan, 1972; Albertville: France, 1992; Turin: Italy, 2006; Grenoble: France, 1968; Beijing: China, 2022; Sarajevo: Yugoslavia, 1984; Lake Placid: USA, 1980; Sochi: Russia, 2014; Innsbruck: Austria, 1964; Squaw Valley: USA, 1960; Nagano: Japan, 1998; Calgary: Canada, 1988; Innsbruck: Austria, 1976; Vancouver: Canada, 2010; PyeongChang: South Korea, 2018

Fashion in the Eighties

Eighties fashion was many things, but subtle wasn't one of them. Brash influences were everywhere from aerobics to Wall Street, from pop princesses to preppy polo shirts. The result was chaotic, but fun. How many eighties throwbacks still lurk in your closet?

Shoulder pads or puffed sleeves

Scrunchies
Patented in 1987 by nightclub singer Rommy Revson, the first scrunchie was designed using the waistband of her pyjama bottoms. The softer alternative to hair bands was named after Revson's dog Scunchie (no, that's not a typo).

Conical bras
Inspired by 1950s bullet bras, Jean Paul Gaultier introduced the cone bra in 1984. As a child he fashioned the bra for his teddy bear; years later he reworked the look for Madonna's Blonde Ambition tour in 1990.

Acid wash jeans

Slogan t-shirts
Designer Katharine Hamnett introduced slogan t-shirts, famously revealing one displaying an anti-nuclear statement when meeting Margaret Thatcher in 1984. Wham opted for 'Choose Life'; for Frankie Goes to Hollywood it was 'Frankie Says Relax'.

Leotards and leg-warmers
Leg-warmers reached the masses following the release of Fame and Flashdance, as well as Jane Fonda exercise videos. Nowadays, leg-warmers are even worn by babies while they have their nappies changed.

Deely boppers, bangle earrings or a polka dot hair bow

Pedal pushers or leggings

Guyliner

Levi 501s

Pixie boots

Ra-ra skirt and PVC belts

Dr Martens
Dr Martens were designed by a German soldier to aid the recovery of his broken foot. Pete Townshend of The Who was the first rock star to wear the boots on stage, and the shoe was adopted by numerous subcultures.

World Buildings

Buildings that are known the world over for all the right (and the wrong) reasons and were opened before you turned 40.

1955	**Hiroshima Peace Museum, Hiroshima** Built following the atomic bombing of Hiroshima as an enduring symbol of peace and to educate, the museum receives over a million visitors each year.
1958	Tokyo Tower, Tokyo
1958	Expo '58 World's Fair, Brussels
1958	Seagram Building, New York
1959	**The Guggenheim, New York** Architect Frank Lloyd Wright produced over 700 sketches of the museum. Upon opening, Woody Allen commented that it looked like a giant lavatory basin.
1961	**Space Needle, Seattle** Built for the 1962 World's Fair. Early shape designs included a tethered balloon and a cocktail shaker before the iconic final design was chosen.
1968	Madison Square Garden, New York City, New York
1969	John Hancock Center, Chicago
1973	Sears Tower, Chicago, Illinois
1973	World Trade Center, New York
1973	**Sydney Opera House, Sydney** The estimated cost for the construction was AU$7m (£4m). It ended up costing AU$102m (£59m), and took 14 years to build rather than the four years planned.
1976	CN Tower, Toronto
1977	Pompidou Centre, Paris
1981	Sydney Tower, Sydney
1990	Washington National Cathedral, Washington DC
1983	**Trump Tower, New York** How many floors there are in Trump Tower? An easy question, right? It was built with 58 floors. But Trump wasn't happy… the ceilings are high on some floors, so the numbers jump from the 6th to the 13th floor. Now it has 68!
1988	Parliament House, Canberra

Grand Designs

Governments around the world spent much of the 20th century nation building (and rebuilding). Here is a selection of striking civil engineering achievements between the ages of 0 and 30.

1955	Disneyland Castle, Anaheim, California
1955	Battersea Power Station, London
1959	**M1 Motorway, London & Leeds** The M1 was the second motorway built in the UK, and it was the first motorway to join two cities. The first section opened in 1959, and the most recent section was added in 1999.
1959	Kariba Dam, Kariba
1962	Butlins, Minehead
1965	Mont Blanc Tunnel, France & Italy
1965	Zeeland Bridge, Netherlands
1966	**Almondsbury Interchange, Bristol & Gloucester** The Almondsbury Interchange was the first example of a four-level stack in the UK, and remains one of only three of its kind in the country.
1967	**Second Blackwall Tunnel, London** The second Blackwall tunnel is relatively straight, unlike the first which is curved. That was to avoid a sewer, but also reportedly so that horses (the main means of transport when built) didn't see daylight at the other end and bolt.
1969	Humber Refinery, Northern Lincolnshire
1970	Aswan Dam, Aswan
1970	Hyde Park Barracks, London
1971	**Spaghetti Junction, Birmingham** Officially the Gravelly Hill Interchange, Spaghetti Junction was named by the Guinness Book of World Records as 'the most complex interchange on the British road system'.
1973	Bosphorus Bridge, Istanbul
1976	**Sonnenberg Tunnel, Lucerne** A 5,000 ft road tunnel that was built to double up as a nuclear shelter for up to 20,000 people. Blast doors at the entrance weigh 350 tons...but take 24 hours to close.

Household Goods in 1987

The shelves, fridges and freezers are piled high with convenience foods. What did we do with all that extra time we'd saved? First, dig out the indigestion tablets. Then tackle a spot of DIY and finally move house, it seems!

Squash racket
The classic eighties sport. Prince Philip played squash to relax while Queen Elizabeth II was in labour with Prince Charles.

Muesli
Spaghetti
Jam doughnuts
Swiss roll
Beefburgers
Mince
Garlic sausage
Frozen prawns
Brie
Red Leicester
Originally called Leicestershire Cheese, the cheese was renamed Red Leicester after World War II to differentiate it from 'White Leicester' made during rationing when the use of colouring agents was banned.

Conifer
Frozen curry and rice
Fish and chips
Synonymous with British cuisine and described by Winston Churchill as 'the good companions', fish and chips were exempt from rationing during World War II, as the government feared any limitations would damage the morale of the nation.

VHS recorder
Ready mixed filler
Home telephone
The popularity of mobile phones has led to a decrease of landlines. Only 73% of British households had a landline used to make calls in 2020.

Fabric conditioner
Estate agent fees
Indigestion tablets

Books of the Decade

By our forties, most of us have decided what we like to read. But occasionally a book can break the spell, revealing the delights of other genres. Did any of these newly published books do that for you?

1991	Regeneration by Pat Barker
1991	**American Psycho by Bret Easton Ellis** Ellis received death threats on account of the violent and misogynistic content. He had to indemnify his publisher from being sued by his family if he were murdered.
1992	The Secret History by Donna Tartt
1992	All the Pretty Horses by Cormac McCarthy
1992	The English Patient by Michael Ondaatje
1993	The Shipping News by E Annie Proulx
1993	Birdsong by Sebastian Faulks
1993	Paddy Clarke Ha Ha Ha by Roddy Doyle
1994	A Suitable Boy by Vikram Seth
1994	Snow Falling on Cedars by David Guterson
1995	A Fine Balance by Rohinton Mistry
1996	Infinite Jest by David Foster Wallace
1996	**A Game of Thrones by George RR Martin** The idea for the story came to Martin as a child through his pet turtles. They lived in a toy castle, and he pretended they were kings, lords and knights.
1996	Bridget Jones's Diary by Helen Fielding
1997	**Harry Potter And The Philosopher's Stone by J K Rowling** In the film of the book, Rik Mayall played the part of Peeves the Poltergeist. The scene was cut before release.
1997	American Pastoral by Philip Roth
1997	The God of Small Things by Arundhati Roy
1997	Underworld by Don DeLillo
1997	Memoirs of a Geisha by Arthur Golden
1997	Blindness by José Saramago
1998	The Poisonwood Bible by Barbara Kingsolver
1999	Being Dead by Jim Crace
2000	White Teeth by Zadie Smith
2000	The Blind Assassin by Margaret Atwood

US Vice Presidents in Your Lifetime

The linchpin of a successful presidency, a springboard to become POTUS, or both? Here are the men - and the woman - who have shadowed the most powerful person in the world in your lifetime. (President in brackets.)

1949-53	**Alben W Barkley** (Harry S Truman) Barkley died of a heart attack during a convention speech three years after the end of his term.
1953-61	Richard Nixon (Dwight Eisenhower)
1961-63	Lyndon B Johnson (John F Kennedy)
1965-69	**Hubert Humphrey** (Lyndon Johnson) Christmas 1977: with just weeks to live, the former VP made goodbye calls. One was to Richard Nixon, the man who had beaten Humphrey to become president in 1968. Sensing Nixon's unhappiness at his status as Washington outcast, Humphrey invited him to take a place of honour at the funeral he knew was fast approaching.
1969-73	**Spiro Agnew (right)**
1973-74	Gerald Ford
1974-77	Nelson Rockefeller
1977-81	Walter Mondale
1981-89	**George HW Bush** He is only the second vice president to win the presidency while holding the office of vice president.
1989-93	**Dan Quayle** You say potato, Quayle said potatoe: he famously told a student to add an 'e' during a 1992 school visit.
1993-2001	**Al Gore** Gore won the Nobel Peace Prize in 2007. Two others have won: Teddy Roosevelt (1906) and Charles Dawes (1925).
2001-09	Dick Cheney
2009-17	Joe Biden
2017-20	**Mike Pence** In the 90s, Pence worked as a conservative talk show host.
2020-	Kamala Harris

Spiro Agnew resigned in 1973, the second VP to quit in America's history (the first was John Calhoun in 1932). He stepped down after being charged with tax evasion and taking bribes. He covered his legal debts with a loan from friend Frank Sinatra. In 1983, Agnew was compelled to repay $268,000: the money he had taken in bribes, plus interest.

Stamps in the Seventies

By the seventies, any hobbyist intent on keeping a complete ongoing collection needed deep pockets (or a rich uncle). New stamps were churned out several times a year and the subjects became ever more esoteric: not just flowers and trees but racket sports, or paintings of horse races. Was your album gathering dust by then?

1970	Commonwealth Games
1971	British rural architecture
1972	Polar explorers
1972	Village churches
1972	Royal Silver Wedding celebration
1973	Plant a Tree Year
1973	County Cricket
1973	**400th anniversary of the birth of Inigo Jones** Not a household name by today's standards, Jones was an early and influential architect. He designed Covent Garden Square and parts of St Paul's Cathedral.
1973	Royal Wedding (Princess Anne and Mark Phillips)
1973	Britain's entry into the EC
1974	Medieval Warriors
1975	Sailing
1975	100 years since the birth of Jane Austen
1976	100 years of the telephone
1976	**British cultural traditions** The four chosen were a Morris dancer, a Scots piper, a Welsh harpist and an Archdruid.
1977	Racket sports
1977	Silver Jubilee
1977	Wildlife
1978	**Energy resources** In an era before renewable energy the choices made were oil, coal, natural gas and electricity.
1978	Horses
1979	Dogs
1979	Spring wild flowers
1979	Paintings of horse races
1979	150 years of the Metropolitan Police

More Things People Do Now...

... that nobody ever did when you were small – because they couldn't, wouldn't, or definitely shouldn't!

✦ **Place a bet *during* a sporting event**
This became popular in the 1990s; first on the phone, now online.

✦ Turn on underfloor heating

✦ **Buy soft toilet rolls**
In 1942, a wonder was created in Walthamstow's St Andrews Road, one for which the bottoms of the world owe a huge debt: two-ply, soft toilet roll ('It's splinter-free'!). It was christened Andrex.

✦ Talk to a smart speaker

✦ Clean up dog poo (not doing it has been an offence since 1996)

✦ Listen to a podcast

✦ **Do a Sudoku puzzle**
How many Japanese words do you know? Tsunami? Karaoke? Sake? In 2005, you likely added another: Sudoku (meaning 'single number'). The puzzle originated in the USA – but was popularised by Wayne Gould, a Hong Kong judge from New Zealand who found a translated version in a Tokyo bookshop.

✦ **Cheat in a pub quiz**
Which two capital cities mean the same in different languages? Who knows? Google knows, and a quick trip to the loo (phone in hand) is a modern phenomenon. (The answer is Sierra Leone's Freetown and Gabon's Libreville – but of course you knew that.)

✦ Order something for same day delivery

✦ Use chopsticks

✦ Fly a drone

✦ **Never watch live TV**
Owning a TV but not watching any live programmes (just streamed content) might sound odd. But that is the reality for many – and around 1.5m have ditched the TV completely.

✦ Eat in the street

✦ Buy water

✦ **Use SatNav**
In the 1980s, Ronald Reagan permitted civilian use of satellites for navigation and opened up a world in which we never need to get lost again – unless we want to. Or the USA pulls the plug.

✦ Argue for hours with strangers you'll never meet

A Lifetime of Progress

It's easy to lose sight of the breadth and pace of life-enhancing inventions made as you grew up – although some of these didn't stand the test of time! These are the biggies before you turned 50.

1973	Mobile phone
1976	Apple Computer
1979	Barcodes
1979	Compact disc
1982	**Emoticons**

The inventor of the smiley emoticon hands out 'Smiley' cookies every Sept 19th – the anniversary of its first use.

1983	Internet
1983	Microsoft Word
1984	LCD projector
1984	Apple Macintosh
1985	Atomic force microscope
1985	**Sinclair C5**

Despite a body and a chassis designed by Lotus and assembled by Hoover, the ahead-of-its-time Sinclair C5 was plagued with problems including poor battery life, the inability to climb gentle hills and safety concerns.

1986	Mir Space Station
1988	**Internet virus**

The first Internet worm (ie self-replicating) was designed to go after passwords. Its inventor was the son of the man who invented... computer passwords.

1989	World Wide Web
1990	Hubble space telescope
1991	Websites
1994	Bluetooth
1995	Mouse with scroll wheel
1996	DVD player
1998	Google
1999	Wi-Fi
2000	Camera phone
2001	Wikipedia

FA Cup Winners Since You Were Born

Many fans have waited decades to see their team lift the cup; many more are still waiting. Here are the teams that have hoisted the trophy in your lifetime (last win in brackets).

Blackpool ⚽ (1952-53)
Newcastle United ⚽ (1954-55)
Aston Villa ⚽ (1956-57)

After Aston Villa won the final in 1895, the FA Cup was stolen from a shop window display in Birmingham. The thief confessed 63 years later, stating he had melted the trophy down to make coins.

Bolton Wanderers ⚽ (1957-58)
Nottingham Forest ⚽ (1958-59)
Wolverhampton Wanderers ⚽ (1959-60)
West Bromwich Albion ⚽ (1967-68)
Leeds United ⚽ (1971-72)
Sunderland ⚽ (1972-73)
Southampton ⚽ (1975-76)
Ipswich Town ⚽ (1977-78)
West Ham United ⚽ (1979-80)
Coventry City ⚽ (1986-87)
Wimbledon ⚽ (1987-88)

Wimbledon shocked the country in 1988 when they beat First Division champions Liverpool in the FA Cup final, overcoming 17-1 odds.

Tottenham Hotspur ⚽ (1990-91)
Everton ⚽ (1994-95)
Liverpool ⚽ (2005-06)
Portsmouth ⚽ (2007-08)
Wigan Athletic ⚽ (2012-13)
Manchester United ⚽ (2015-16)
Chelsea ⚽ (2017-18)

Former Chelsea and Ivory Coast striker Didier Drogba is the only player to score in four separate FA Cup Finals.

Manchester City ⚽ (2018-19)
Arsenal ⚽ (2019-20)
Leicester City ⚽ (2020-21)

Gameshow Hosts of the Seventies and Eighties

What do points make? I've started so I'll finish. Shut that door! You can't beat a bit of Bully! The catchphrases echo down the ages from these much-loved TV favourites.

David Vine ►◄ (A Question of Sport)
Stuart Hall ►◄ (It's a Knockout)
Anneka Rice ►◄ (Treasure Hunt)
Kenneth Kendall ►◄ (Treasure Hunt)
Cilla Black ►◄ (Blind Date)
Born Priscilla White, the stage name of Cilla Black came about by mistake. Featured in the first issue of Mersey Beat newspaper, the journalist accidentally called her Cilla Black. Cilla liked the name and opted to keep it.

Barry Cryer ►◄ (Jokers Wild)
Nicholas Parsons ►◄ (Just a Minute, Sale of the Century)
Jim Bowen ►◄ (Bullseye)
After completing his national service in the bomb disposal unit, Jim Bowen worked as a teacher and was promoted to deputy head, but gave up teaching once he appeared on The Comedians alongside Mike Reid.

Mike Read ►◄ (Pop Quiz)
David Coleman ►◄ (A Question of Sport)
Prof. Heinz Wolff ►◄ (The Great Egg Race)
Bob Holness ►◄ (Blockbusters)
Magnus Magnusson ►◄ (Mastermind)
Angela Rippon ►◄ (Masterteam)
Noel Edmonds ►◄ (Telly Addicts)
Noel Edmonds has made headlines for plotting to buy the BBC, starting a pet counselling service, and driving a mannequin called Candice around in his black cab to dissuade the public from trying to flag him down.

Ted Rogers ►◄ (3-2-1)
Terry Wogan ►◄ (Blankety Blank)
Les Dawson ►◄ (Blankety Blank)
Larry Grayson ►◄ (The Generation Game)

Popular Food in the 1980s

Our last trolley dash takes us down the aisle at lunchtime, piled high with eat-on-the-go snacks and sandwiches. Stop on the way home for a deep pan pizza and a Diet Coke; end the day with a slice of Battenberg cake. Congratulations, you've just eaten the eighties!

Crunchy Nut Cornflakes
The cereal was invented in Manchester in 1980. Pity the poor Americans: it took 30 years for Crunchy Nut to cross the Atlantic.

Kellogg's Fruit and Fibre

Prepacked sandwiches
The prepacked sandwich was first sold by M&S in spring 1980. The range was small, conservative, made in-store and used whatever ingredients were plentiful (even if that was pilchards).

Viennetta

Trifle
In 1596, Thomas Dawson recorded the first recipe for trifle in his books, *The Good Huswifes Jewell*. It was essentially thick cream, rosewater, sugar and ginger. Jelly didn't appear until the 1700s.

Chicken Kiev

Vol au vent

Battenberg cake

Pizza
Pizza Hut claim to be the first company to sell food online – one of their signature pizzas via their Pizanet website, back in 1994.

Garlic bread

Kiwi

Sun-dried tomatoes

Potato waffles

Happy Meals

Diet Coke
Within two years of its unveiling in 1982, Diet Coke became the most popular diet soft drink in the world, and the third most popular soft drink overall behind Coca Cola and Pepsi.

Rowntree's Drifters

Hedgehog-flavoured crisps

Burton's fish 'n' chips

Chicken satay

Eighties Symbols of Success

In the flamboyant era of Dallas and Dynasty there were many ways to show that you, too, had really made it. Forty years on, it's fascinating to see how some of these throwbacks are outdated or available to nearly everyone, while others are still reserved for today's wealthy peacocks.

Car phone
Dishwasher
Children at private school
Waterbed
The modern-day waterbed was designed by a US student for his master's thesis project. Original fillings included corn syrup, and then jelly, before he settled on water. They were popular but problematic due to their weight and susceptibility to puncture, as Edward Scissorhands found out.

Second cars
Holidays abroad
Conservatory
Pony
Colour TV
Diamonds
Cordless phone
Birkin bag
A chance encounter between Hermès Executive Chairman Jean-Louis Dumas and Jane Birkin on a plane inspired the Birkin bag. The contents of Birkin's bag spilled out, and Dumas suggested she needed a bag with pockets, so Birkin sketched her idea on a sick bag.

Double glazing
Rolex watch
Leather Filofax
Mont Blanc pen
Newton's Cradle desk toy
Named after Isaac Newton and the cat's cradle, an early version was wooden, expensive and sold at Harrods. Chrome imitations followed. TV programme Myth Busters built a supersized cradle with concrete-filled chrome wrecking balls... it didn't work.

Stone cladding

The first UK car phone call was made in 1959 from outside the Lymm Hotel in Cheshire; human operators were used to connect calls until the 1980s. John Lennon wrote the lyrics for I'm Only Sleeping on the back of a car phone demand letter.

Cars of the 1980s

Many cars you might associate with the eighties were on the road long before then, from the Ford Granada and Escort to the Porsche 911. But this is the decade they arguably hit their stride alongside other automotive icons.

Toyota Corolla
Introduced in 1966, the Toyota Corolla became the best-selling car worldwide by 1974. The car was named after a ring of petals.

Volvo 240

BMW 3 Series

Volkswagen Golf
Sold as the Rabbit in the US and the Caribe in Mexico.

Volkswagen Passat

Vauxhall Astra

Triumph Acclaim

Porsche 911
Originally the Porsche 901 on its 1964 debut, the name was changed after Peugeot claimed they had exclusive rights to naming cars with three digits and a zero in the middle.

Jaguar XJS

Nissan Micra

Peugeot 205

Austin Maestro

Vauxhall Nova
The Vauxhall Nova inspired a series of comical bumper stickers, including 'You've been Novataken', and 'Vauxhall Casanova'. It was called the Corsa everywhere but Britain where it sounded too much like the word 'coarser'. It was renamed anyway in 1993.

Ford Sierra
Neil Kinnock had one of the first Sierras. He wrecked it in a crash.

Austin Montego

Volkswagen Polo

Austin Metro
Promoted with comical adverts, the car became one of the best-selling cars in UK history, and even Princess Diana owned one.

Ford Fiesta
The Fiesta is the UK's best-selling car of all time.

Vauxhall Cavalier

Eighties TV Gameshows

By the eighties, new formats aimed at youngsters – your youngsters? – were introduced. Some shows went digital or took to the skies; others kept it (very) simple, and a few remain family favourites to this day.

The Adventure Game

Treasure Hunt

Blind Date

The pilot episode of Blind Date was hosted by Duncan Norvelle, but he was quickly replaced by Cilla Black. Black presented the entire original run of the series for eighteen years, before unexpectedly announcing her departure on the show's first ever live episode.

Surprise Surprise

Countdown

Catchphrase

Blockbusters

Telly Addicts

3-2-1

The show's mascot and booby prize, Dusty Bin, cost around £10,000 to build. He was built by visual effects engineer Ian Rowley, who also operated Dusty Bin in the studio.

Blankety Blank

Bob's Full House

The instantly recognisable scoreboard was dubbed Mr Babbage by original host Bob Monkhouse. This was a nod to Charles Babbage, the inventor of the first programmable computer. In the reboot, Mr Babbage was replaced with a colour scoreboard, but the original board soon returned.

Bullseye

Cheggers Plays Pop

Family Fortunes

The Great Egg Race

Give Us a Clue

The Krypton Factor

Play Your Cards Right

The Price is Right

The Pyramid Game

Popular Girls' Names

Of the fifty names that made the Top 10 from 1900-74, only four have appeared since: Claire, Emma, Samantha and Sarah. (Oddly, names beginning with 'D' are now a rarity with no Top 10 entries in the last fifty years!)

Amelia
Olivia
Along with other names ending in 'a', Olivia rose to popularity in the late nineties and has remained a favourite ever since. She's been number one or two from 2008 to the present day.

Lily
Jessica
Emily
Sophie
Ruby
Grace
Ava
Isabella
Evie
Chloe
Mia
Poppy
Isla
Ella
Isabelle
Sophia
Freya
Daisy
Charlotte
Maisie
Lucy
Phoebe
Scarlett

Rising and falling stars:
Willow: welcome to the Top 100!
Lexie, Lauren, Rebecca, Tia and Nicole: we're afraid your time is up.

Books of the Decade

Our final decade of books are the bookstore favourites from your fifties. How many did you read...and can you remember the plot, or the cover?

2001	Atonement by Ian McEwan
2001	The Corrections by Jonathan Franzen
2001	Austerlitz by W G Sebald
2001	Life of Pi by Yann Martel
2002	Everything Is Illuminated by Jonathan Safran Foer
2002	**The Lovely Bones by Alice Sebold** At university, Sebold was beaten and sexually assaulted in a location where a girl had previously been murdered. Her experience and her subsequent reactions to it informed a novel called Monsters about the rape and murder of a teenager, later retitled as The Lovely Bones.
2003	**The Kite Runner by Khaled Hosseini** Hosseini was inspired to write the book after watching news about the Taliban, who had banned the sport of kite flying.
2003	Vernon God Little by DBC Pierre
2003	Brick Lane by Monica Ali
2004	The Line of Beauty by Alan Hollinghurst
2004	Cloud Atlas by David Mitchell
2004	Gilead by Marilynne Robinson
2004	Small Island by Andrea Levy
2005	Never Let Me Go by Kazuo Ishiguro
2005	The Book Thief by Markus Zusak
2005	The Girl with the Dragon Tattoo by Stieg Larsson
2005	No Country for Old Men by Cormac McCarthy
2005	Saturday by Ian McEwan
2006	The Road by Cormac McCarthy
2007	A Thousand Splendid Suns by Khaled Hosseini
2007	The Ghost by Robert Harris
2008	The White Tiger by Aravind Adiga
2008	The Hunger Games by Suzanne Collins
2009	Wolf Hall by Hilary Mantel
2009	The Help by Kathryn Stockett
2010	The Hand That First Held Mine by Maggie O'Farrell

April 17 1970: Jim Lovell is brought aboard a helicopter, the last of the
three astronauts from the Apollo 13 mission to be lifted from the floating

Apollo Astronauts

Not all of those who have been to the moon are equally well known. Twelve landed; twelve remained in orbit. Gus Grissom, Ed White, and Roger B Chaffee died in training. BBC and ITV broadcast the Apollo 11 landing live, in the first all-night transmission. The landing was at 9.17pm, but Armstrong didn't take one monumental step until 3.56am.

Landed on the moon:

Alan Bean

Alan Shepard
Shepard was the oldest person to walk on the moon at the age of 47.

Buzz Aldrin

Charles Duke

David Scott

Edgar Mitchell

Eugene Cernan

Harrison Schmitt

James Irwin

John Young

Neil Armstrong

Pete Conrad

Remained in low orbit:

Al Worden

Bill Anders
Anders took the iconic Earthrise photo.

Dick Gordon

Frank Borman

Fred Haise

Jack Swigert

Jim Lovell

Ken Mattingly

Michael Collins

Ron Evans
Made the final spacewalk of the program to retrieve film cassettes.

Stuart Roosa
On the Apollo 14 mission he carried seeds from 5 species of trees. They were planted across the US and are known as Moon Trees.

Tom Stafford

NASA

Popular Boys' Names

60

The most favoured names are now a curious blend of the evergreen (Thomas), the rediscovered (Harry), and those enjoying their first proper outing (Joshua).

Harry
Oliver
Harry took Oliver's crown in 2011, but it was only a loan: Oliver rose back to the top in 2013 and has remained there ever since.

Jack
Alfie
Charlie
Thomas
Jacob
James
Joshua
William
Ethan
George
Riley
Daniel
Samuel
Noah
Oscar
Joseph
Mohammed
Max
Dylan
Muhammad
Alexander
Archie
Benjamin

Rising and falling stars:
While names fell in and out of fashion in great numbers in the eighties and nineties, the pace has slowed. New this year: Logan, Spencer, Noah, Jude and Luca. Out: Josh, Anthony and Marcus.

Things People Did When You Were Growing Up (Part 2)

Finally, here are more of the things we saw, we did and errands we ran as kids that nobody needs, wants, or even understands how to do in the modern age!

+ Drink syrup of figs
+ Preserve vegetables
+ Save the silver chocolate papers from Roses
+ **Eat offal**
  Tripe was never on ration but long out of favour by the time the tripe dresser's fate was sealed in 1992, when BSE broke out.

+ **Make a carbon copy**
  Carbon paper was first patented by Ralph Wedgwood, son of Thomas Wedgwood, in 1806, for his Noctograph – designed to help blind people write without ink. The smell and texture are just a memory, but emails sent in 'cc' (carbon copy) might remind you!

+ **Wash handkerchiefs**
  You'd have to keep (and wash) a hanky for nine years to outweigh the CO_2 emissions of its tissue cousins.

+ Use talcum powder
+ Make a penfriend
+ **Wire a plug**
  Strip and route wires to the terminal; fit the right fuse. Not any more. In 1994, it became illegal to sell appliances without fitted plugs.

+ Darn a hole in your sock
+ Refill your pen from an inkwell
+ Wind on your camera for another shot
+ See the bones in your foot at the shoe shop through a Pedoscope
+ Pluck a chicken
+ **Smoke on a bus**
  'When will this fanaticism going to stop?' asked one MP in 1962, about a proposed ban on lower-deck smoking.

+ Scrape ice patterns off the inside of your bedroom window
+ Service your own car
+ Buy starch or blue bags for your washing
+ **Play Spot the Ball**
  Spot the Ball was launched in 1973. More than 10 years passed without a jackpot winner as its popularity declined.

Printed in Great Britain
by Amazon

83227135R00059